NMG

A NormanMichaelGillerPublishing publication
in association with Terry Baker, of A1 Sporting Speakers
© Norman Giller/Michael Giller/Terry Baker 2010

First published in 2010 by NMG Publishing
PO Box 3386, Ferndown, BH22 8XT

10 9 8 7 6 5 4 3 2 1

A CIP catalogue for this title is available from the British Library
ISBN 978-0-9543243-6-0
Typeset and designed by NMG Enterprises, Dorset, UK
Printed and bound in the United Kingdom by Antony Rowe Limited
Bumper's Farm, Chippenham, Wiltshire SN14 6LH

*Co-author Norman Giller recommends the official Chelsea club website
as a mine of information and entertainment ... www.chelseafc.com*

CHOPPER'S CHELSEA

BLUES LEGEND RON HARRIS TURNS SELECTOR

RON HARRIS with **Norman Giller**

Statistics Michael Giller, Illustrations Art Turner

Introduced by
JIMMY GREAVES and **Terry Baker**

NMG

Authors Ron Harris and Norman Giller
dedicate this book to the memory
of their old mate and genius
of a Chelsea footballer
PETER OSGOOD

CHOPPER'S CHELSEA: Contents

JUST the name 'Chopper' Harris brings me out in bruises. He kicked lumps out of me over a period of more than ten years, and here I am paying bloody tribute to him in his latest book! Somehow we have become good pals since he stopped literally marking me, and he is a regular and popular guest on my roadshows organised by our mutual pal and agent, Terry Baker.

There's a myth that Ron would not have lasted ten minutes in today's sanitised, don't-touch-me-or-I'll-fall-over game. Rubbish. He wouldn't get past five minutes.

I first got to know Chopper when he was starting out as an apprentice at Stamford Bridge. I was an old man of 19 already established in the Chelsea first-team, and I remember that he treated me with the respect I deserved in our kick arounds. "Oi, Greavsie, you going to let anybody else have the f*****g ball, you greedy git ..."

I had moved on to Milan and then Tottenham by the time he became a fixture in the Chelsea defence. Everytime we played against each other he used to stick to me like shit to a blanket. He was without question the most disciplined, determined (and sometimes downright dirty) man marker I faced throughout my career.

He was a stone-faced git, who would not allow himself to get involved in the friendly, on-pitch banter I used to like to have with my opponents. I remember saying to him once, "I bet if I went for a crap you'd come in there with me."

"No I bloody wouldn't," he replied. "But I'd be waiting at the door for you when you came out."

Ron's well-earned reputation as a hard man tended to overshadow the fact that he could play the game a bit. He used to tidy up at the back and in midfield and then unselfishly give the ball to players he knew could use it better than him, the likes of Terry Venners, then Cookie and Alan Hudson. I'm sure they appreciate that he helped make them seem better players with his accurate service.

He was Chelsea's most loyal and dedicated servant in the club's history, and nobody is ever going to beat his long-playing record. I have got to like Ron a lot, but deep down I will always think what a horrible bastard he was to play against. He played when football was a man's game of physical contact. No player ever made stronger contact. Enjoy his book and his selections. I found them fascinating, and I am too much of a chicken to disagree with any of them. The old Chopper is still in there somewhere!

Jim Greaves

Terry Baker, entrepreneur and agent, with his client and good mate Chopper

BECAUSE of his fearsome reputation as an on-pitch assassin, I wondered what sort of animal I was going to find when I met Ron Harris for the first time. What a pleasant surprise! Instead of a snapping, snarling Rottweiler I found something of a pussycat! Sorry Ron, if this dents your hardman image.

What you see with Ron is what you get. He is polite, fanatical about being punctual, swears a lot but knows when to control his tongue, is always smart without ever being flash, does not suffer fools gladly, has a sharp, dry sense of humour, and is one of the most loyal and dependable guys walking this earth. What his fellow-Cockneys call 'a diamond geezer.'

It is my pleasure and privilege to represent many leading Golden Oldie sports stars – ranging from Greavsie to Pele, Henry Cooper to Frank Bruno, and Ricky Hatton to Ricky Villa. They are all great professionals, but some others have to be prodded and continually nagged to be on time for events and appearances.

Ron is always there on the dot, does his duties professionally and conscientiously, and is always keen to give of his best.

That also sums up how Ron was as a footballer. It is legend at the Bridge how he was always early for kick-offs and ready and eager to go, and once on the pitch there was no more focused (and fierce) competitor who always gave 100 per cent and then more.

Because of his reputation for not taking prisoners with his tackling, it tends to be forgotten that Ron had complete mastery of the ball and he made the team tick with his energy and enthusiasm in midfield or at the back, wherever he was needed most.

His astonishing Chelsea appearances record says it all about his dedication to duty ... 655 League games over a span of sixteen years.

I am delighted to publish this book in harness with the father-and-son team – Norman and Michael Giller – who between them have enough sports statistical knowledge to sink the Titanic. Norman reported Ron's career from day one when he was chief football writer for the *Daily Express*. He has transferred Ron's views to paper, and between them – Chopper Harris and Team Giller – they have come up with a compelling and at times controversial book that no true-Blue Chelsea fan will want to miss. Enjoy!

Terry Baker

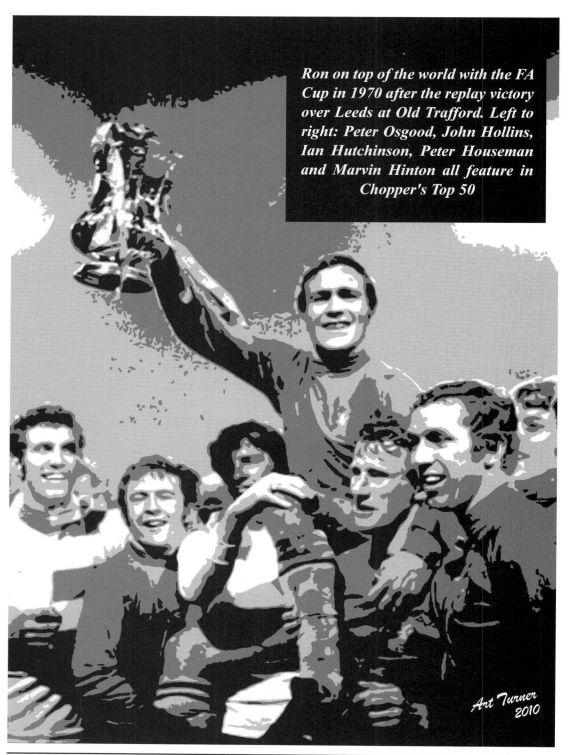

Ron on top of the world with the FA Cup in 1970 after the replay victory over Leeds at Old Trafford. Left to right: Peter Osgood, John Hollins, Ian Hutchinson, Peter Houseman and Marvin Hinton all feature in Chopper's Top 50

Art Turner
2010

CHOPPER'S CHELSEA: *The Hard Game by Ron Harris*

THIS selecting lark is the hardest game of all! When my old sparring partner Norman Giller invited me to pick the 50 greatest Chelsea players from the last 50 years I thought it would be a doddle. Wrong! It was not which players to pick that was so difficult as deciding which ones to leave out. My choices go back to when I first started getting my kicks with Chelsea in the late 1950s, and if I have missed anybody obvious I apologise. Put it down to the fact that I am now officially an old git.

I won't bullshit. I am proud of the reputation I had for being one of football's hard nuts. When I played, it was a real man's game of physical contact. Tackling was one of the arts, and I like to think I was a master at it. In the modern game if you breathe on a player it can bring you a yellow or even a red card for challenges that in my day were part and parcel of football.

I watched the World Cup in South Africa on the box and could not believe the theatrics and tantrums over tackles that would have been considered soft in the school playground when I was a kid growing up in London. Players were going down as if shot the moment an opponent went near them. It made a mockery of what they were calling the greatest football show on earth.

Then, in the Final between Spain and Holland, I could hardly believe my eyes. It was suddenly like watching Leeds of the Seventies, as the Dutch players dived in with challenges as if they should have been wearing their traditional clogs. Some of the tackles would even have been considered a bit strong in the good old bad old days when we literally played the game for kicks. As my old foe-turned-friend Greavsie would say, it's a funny old game.

I enjoyed the best years of my life at the Bridge. It was like a second home from 1959 until 1980, and I think I am better qualified than most to pick the greatest Chelsea players of the last 50 years. You are, I know, going to disagree with some of my choices, but opinions make the world go round. If you want an argument meet me behind the the old Shed and we will sort it out. Joking, of course.

Mind you, I had a few opponents I would liked to have taken behind the old Shed to sort them out. I had the reputation of being a tough and rough man, but I usually tried to play within the rules and my 'Chopper' nickname didn't help. But there were several players from my generation who were craftily nasty, slipping in painful little ankle taps

Chopper and John Boyle ride shotgun on the one and only George Best

and going over the top when tackling. Whatever anybody says about the way I played the game, they would have to concede that I was all up front. I suppose you could say I was an honest villain. PLayers knew where they stood (or fell) with me.

The facts of this book are Norman Giller's, while the *feelings* are mine. Norm and I go back a long way. He was a bit of a Jack the lad when I first knew him, and he preferred the company of the celebrity players like Venners and Georgie Graham than a serious git like me. One of his exclusives for the *Express* – which in those days was always my paper of choice – was when Tommy Docherty stripped Terry Venables of the Chelsea captaincy and made me, at 22, the youngest skipper in the club's history. The Doc went potty when Norman got hold of the story, and he asked him not to print it until he had told Terry. Norm explained that the story had already gone to press, so Tommy had to ring Venners at home that evening and tell him he was getting the chop as captain. Happy days.

I have got some thank yous to make before I get on with the selecting game. First of all, ta very much to Greavsie for his introduction. We have great fun on stage together these days recalling our feuds on the football field. Jimbo rarely got the better of me, as I will reveal when I make my assessment of him. He was, of course, a shoe-in for a place in my top 50.

Thanks to Terry Baker, entrepreneur and proprietor of A1 Sporting Speakers and A1 Sporting Memorabilia. He is a top man and is the motivator who got this book on the road. He and his wife/partner Freda have an impressive stable of sporting stars, and I am flattered and pleased to be among them.

Most of all I have to thank 'Know-all' Norm, who has expertly ghosted my opinions on to the page. He has cleverly brought up his son, Michael, as a clone, and his stats and facts give a special lift to the book and will, I know, be appreciated and enjoyed by the Chelsea faithful.

Terry, Freda, Norman, Michael and I all live in dozy, delightful Dorset, and it is a pleasure for me to be working with them on this project that I hope will revive good memories for Stamford Bridge fans. I've always had a special relationship with them.

Norman was particularly close to our mutual old mate, Peter Osgood, and we agreed that this book should be dedicated to his memory. Of the fifty players featured on the following pages he was probably the most naturally gifted. If Ossie had been playing today his transfer value would be fifty million-plus. Yes, he was that special.

I hope you join me in the selecting game. You need to know the rules. The players have had to have played for Chelsea during the last 50 years, which takes us back to when I first signed as a pro at the Bridge. This knocks out such Chelsea legends as Roy Bentley, John Harris, Derek Saunders and Jim Lewis. In fact the only player who makes it from the '55 Championship squad is Frank Blunstone, who was still playing for the Blues when I first got into the League team.

Another important rule to remember is that each player has had to have played in a minimum 150 League and Cup games for Chelsea. This, of course, eliminates a lot of the modern greats who have graced the Bridge but have not hung around too long in an era when loyalty does not count as much as in the old days.

I will be surprised if anybody stays at the Bridge long enough to beat my appearances record of 655 League matches and 795 games in total. Bloody hell, no wonder I feel knackered these days!

Tell you what, wish I could do it all again. Mind you, I would have to play a different sort of game in this modern era when players fall over if you cough near them. I was no saint when I was playing, but in my own way I always played the game fairly. I never cheated, went down without being touched, or tried to con referees into giving penalties or into taking the names of opponents.

I played under seven different managers at Chelsea after being signed as an apprentice by Ted Drake. Tommy Doc gave me my first call-up and I was later selected by Dave Sexton, Ron Suart, Eddie McCreadie, Ken Shellito, Danny Blanchflower and Geoff Hurst. Never once did I go to any of them and ask for a transfer or even a rise. I just got on with my job, and nobody was prouder than me to captain Chelsea.

All these years later, I remain a true Blue blood, and hope my selections stir memories for you of some of the great players who have been heroes at the Bridge. Their personal quotes have been quarried from either the memories of Norman or me or the archives, and the stats are all the work of Michael Giller, a chip off the old Giller block.

Norman reported my career when with the *Daily Herald* and then the *Daily Express*. He rarely had a good word to say for me, preferring to suck up to his mates like Venners and Ossie. I'll forgive him if this book sells well.

I am presenting my choices in the order that the players were born, and I then put myself through more torture by picking two Chelsea teams to face each other in a dream game – British Chelsea against Overseas Chelsea. Perhaps Chelsea v Chelski would be the best way to put it.

I think you will find this a very select book. If you like it, tell your friends. If you don't, tell me – if you dare :-)

Thanks for your company. Now eyes down, and start playing the selecting game with me.

CHOPPER'S CHELSEA: *The Ron Harris File*

Born Hackney, 13 November 1944.

Capped by England at schoolboy, youth and Under-23 level. Captain of the England youth team that won the 'Little World Cup' at Wembley in 1963.

Followed his older brother, Alan, to Stamford Bridge to become an apprentice professional in 1959.

Stayed at the Bridge for 21 years, playing a club record 655 League games (9 of them as a substitute). Scored 13 goals.

Played 64 FA Cup ties, 48 League Cup, 27 European club matches and one Charity Shield game for an all-time Chelsea appearances record of 795 matches.

Joined Brentford in May 1980, and played 61 matches for the Griffin Park club, including one substitute appearance.

At 22, he was Chelsea's youngest club captain. When he led Chelsea out for the 1967 FA Cup final against Tottenham at Wembley he was then the youngest captain in FA Cup final history.

Captained the Chelsea team that beat Leeds in the 1970 FA Cup final replay at Old Trafford, and skippered the side that collected the 1971 European Cup Winners' Cup by beating Real Madrid in a replay in Athens.

Born: Crewe, October 17 1934

Career span: 1952-1963

Clubs: Crewe (1952-53)
48 League games, 12 goals
Chelsea (1953-63)
317 League games, 47 goals

Won England schoolboys, youth, Under-23 and five full England caps

Chelsea honours: League championship medal (1954-55)

FRANK was at the fag-end of his playing career when I joined Chelsea as an apprentice in 1959, and had lost half a yard of speed after suffering a broken leg. But you could still see he had been a real quality player, who at his peak was a jet-paced left-winger who could take any defence apart with a mix of speed and dribbling skill – the sort of bloke I would have been looking to chip over the touchline had he been trying his tricks on me.

You ever play that Monty Python 'We were so poor' game, when you you make out you were poorer than anybody else? Frank had us all beaten by a mile on that one, only he wasn't exaggerating. He was one of thirteen children brought up in wartime poverty in Crewe.

He was an outstanding schoolboy footballer, even though he never owned a pair of proper boots until he had been called up for trials. Frank told us how he used to play with a borrowed boot on his favourite left foot, with his everyday shoe on his right. Wearing a proper pair of boots, he made it into the England schoolboy squad that included the soon-to-be-great Johnny Haynes.

Frank kicked off his professional career with his local club Crewe at the age of sixteen, turning down the chance to join the Cullis Cubs at Wolves. He started out as a scheming inside-left before finding his best role as a probing outside-left. It was soon obvious that he was far too good for the Third Division North circuit, and Chelsea came calling with a then massive cheque of £7,500.

The eighteen-year-old kid from Crewe joined Chelsea at the back end of the 1952-53 season, and helped them beat relegation by just one point. He quickly established himself as a key player, and played a prominent part in Chelsea's shock League championship triumph in 1954-55, in between doing his National Service with the Army.

By then he was a regular in the England Under-23s side, and – with Duncan Edwards helping himself to a hat-trick as a makeshift centre-forward – gave a devastating performance in a 6-0 slaughter of Scotland. Frank liked playing against the Jocks. In April 1955 he was a wizard on the wing as England powered to a 7-2 victory.

He had won the first of his five caps in a 3-2 win over Wales, laying on two of Chelsea skipper Roy Bentley's three goals.

His broken leg brought a premature end to his international career, but he continued to serve Chelsea well as the club tried to recapture the League title with a bunch of kids that became known as Drake's Ducklings.

Frank was one of the older players, yet still in his 20s. One of the stunning stars was a prolific goal scorer called Jimmy Greaves, who famously said of Blunstone: "He has the heart the size of a cabbage."

I came on the Stamford Bridge scene as the Ted Drake reign was rolling to an end. New coach Tommy Docherty took a shine to me, and quickly put me into his team when he became the new manager in 1962. We bounced straight back up after being relegated and Frank continued to bomb down the wing, this time with the young and hungry Bobby Tambling as his partner.

Frank Blunstone, heart as big as a cabbage

Frank was enjoying his Indian Summer out on the wing, but his career was virtually finished by a second broken leg, and he switched to coaching at the Bridge before managing Brentford. He then joined Tommy Doc as assistant manager at Manchester United and later Derby County, where he had a short spell in charge.

QUOTE UNQUOTE: Frank Blunstone

"They were wonderful days at the Bridge. We played football that was carefree and unpredictable. You could always hear the sound of laughter in our dressing-room, and you could warm your hands on the club spirit. The Championship season was as unexpected to us as everybody else in the game, and there were times when we played quality football that surprised even us. I just wish the League had not stopped us going into Europe. That would've been an interesting adventure!"

Born: Greenwich, November 8 1937

Career span: 1955-70

**Clubs: Chelsea (1955-62)
251 League games, 47 goals
West Ham (1962-68)
167 League games, 33 goals
Leyton Orient (1968-70)
72 League games, 6 goals**

England youth, 9 Under-23 and 3 full England caps

PETER was seventeen when he joined Chelsea from Ford United at the back end of the 1954-55 season, and was pitched straight into the team for the final shots of the League championship season. He played just three times, so did not qualify for a medal.

A fast, tricky right-winger, he was hailed as the 'new' Stanley Matthews and gave many full-backs the runaround in the days when most teams played two direct wingers

He was one of the established first-team players when I followed my brother Alan to the Bridge in 1959, so I used to have to clean his boots and pick up his dirty gear after him. Welcome to the glamorous world of professional football.

I used to mark him in training matches and can vouch for the fact that he was quick and clever. He was good enough to play three times for England, with his first cap coming in the 1958 World Cup finals match against the USSR in Sweden. Ron Greenwood, who was in the Chelsea squad as a centre-half when Peter first arrived at the Bridge, always admired his style of wing play. But Tommy Doc did not fancy him much when he took over as manager in 1962, and quickly bombed him out to Greenwood, who by then was managing West Ham. The fee was around thirty-five grand, which was quite big in those days.

Peter helped the Bobby Moore-captained West Ham team win the FA Cup and European Cup Winners' Cup in back-to-back seasons before winding down his injury-hit career at Orient. He became a coach at the West Ham youth academy, bringing on among others a youngster called Joe Cole. I heard a story that Joe later quietly paid Peter's medical expenses when he had to have specialist surgery. So not all today's pros are just money-grabbing mercenaries. Well done, Joe.

QUOTE UNQUOTE: Peter Brabrook

"If only our defence had been as consistent as our attack, we could have won the League title again while I was at the Bridge. But we used to often let in more goals in a season than we scored, which was frustrating. The Drake Ducklings were great going forward but always dodgy in defence."

Born: Norwood, February 2 1940
Career span: 1957-74

Clubs: Charlton (1957-63)
131 League games, 2 goals
Chelsea (1963-74)
265 League games, 3 goals

Won 3 England U-23 caps

Chelsea honours: League Cup winners' medal (1965), FA Cup runners-up (1967), FA Cup winners' medal (1970 as a substitute)

A LOT of Chelsea supporters don't know who we old pros are talking about when we mention the name Lou, and we have to explain at forums that we mean Marvin Hinton. We nicknamed him Lou after the well-known London ticket spiv 'One-Arm Lou', who with the likes of Fat Stan Flashman and Johnny the Stick were among the Del Boy-type characters who used to trade match tickets, many of which they'd got from players on the old hush-hush.

Marvin was a lovely bloke who was always chasing ticket deals, and the 'Lou' nickname just stuck after he had joined us from Charlton as one of Tommy Doc's major buys after he had taken over as manager from Ted Drake.

Lou not only brought his likeable personality but also a good footballing brain to the Bridge. For years we had been giving away too many goals, and the Doc set about tightening the defence, and in Lou – okay, Marvin – he had found a player who was equally at home at full-back or, his best position, centre-half. He had a cool head in a crisis and would dribble the ball out of defence and pass it in a constructive manner. This used to frighten the life out of the fans who would shout, "Get rid of the f***** thing." But Lou knew what he was doing and would usually manage to set up a counter-attack. He was almost in the Bobby Moore class in the way he could control the ball and then bring the forwards into play – but only almost, because for me Mooro was THE master defender.

Marvin and I were full-back partners when Chelsea won their first trophy under the Doc – the 1965 Football League Cup. We beat Leicester City – Gordon Banks and all – in a two-leg final, winning 3-2 at the Bridge and then holding on for a goalless draw at Filbert Street.

The mid-60s were his peak years and Alf Ramsey named him in his provisional 40-man squad for the 1966 World Cup finals, but he did not make the last cut and was, in my opinion, unlucky not to add a full cap to the three he won with the Under-23s while with Charlton.

By the time the 1970 FA Cup run came around, Marvin had been troubled by recurring injuries and became second choice in the centre of the defence when John Dempsey arrived from Fulham.

He picked up an FA Cup winners' medal against Leeds as our substitute – coming on late in both games – and was a non-playing member of the squad when we picked up the Cup Winners' Cup against Real Madrid in Athens the following season. Typical of his pride in the club, he was as happy for us as if he had played in the final himself.

Staying with the club until he was in his mid-30s, Marvin was a valuable older statesman who helped bring on young players in the reserves, where his ability as a play-anywhere defender came in handy as a cover for the four back-line positions. He later wound down his career playing non-League football with Barnet.

After he hung up his boots, he became a partner in a removals business in Crawley, leaving behind memories of a player who was not only a fine and fair footballer but an asset to the team with his good humour, quiet determination and professional attitude.

QUOTE UNQUOTE: Marvin Hinton

"I loved every moment of my time with Chelsea. They were a great set of blokes, and we had lots of good times on and off the pitch. My only regret is I didn't make it into the England squad for the 1966 World Cup finals. That was a dream for me, but at least Alf Ramsey paid me the compliment of placing me in his 40-man provisional squad. The Chelsea supporters were always fantastic in getting behind us, and I apologise for giving any of them heart attacks with the way I used to play the ball out of defence."

WHERE to begin with Greavsie? I think it best to first lay out his phenomenal goal-scoring record ...

Born East Ham 20 February 1940 Career span: 1957-71

357 goals in the First Division, an all-time record that will never be beaten because the division no longer exists. **44 goals** in 57 England matches, just five behind the all-time record of Bobby Charlton in 106 appearances.

SIX TIMES First Division leading marksman, another record

SEVEN First Division hat-tricks, **SIX** hat-tricks for England.

124 League goals for Chelsea (1957-61), then a club record.

220 League goals for Tottenham (1961-70), still a club record.

13 goals for West Ham (1970-71), **9** goals for AC Milan (1961)

35 goals in the FA Cup, and top scorer for his club in **12** of the 14 seasons in which he played in the First Division.

266 goals in 379 Tottenham matches.

491 goals in all matches at the time of his retirement from League football in 1971 at the all-too early age of 31, and not counting the dozens of goals he scored in non-League football.

AS GREAVSIE said in his introduction to this book, we are now good pals and I often join him in his stage roadshow. What he didn't say– and I love winding him up with this fact – is that in the dozen times I played against him he scored just one goal. Game, set and match to me, Jim

Hands up time, I will admit that he was one of the most difficult opponents I ever faced, and I always had to focus for the full 90 minutes to keep him under lock and key. Let's be honest, there have been few better goalscorers in the history of the game, and I am as proud as punch of my record against him.

I'm just relieved I did not have to mark him in his days with Chelsea when I reckon he was at his brilliant best. We apprentice pros at the Bridge used to cheer ourselves hoarse as we watched him banging in goals left, right and centre ... three times scoring five in a match and hat-tricks by the bucketload.

Any fans from my generation will tell you that the spiky-haired kid at Chelsea was the finest finisher of them all. He was a genius at unbalancing defenders and, if you look at old photos of him scoring, you will always see opponents sitting on their arses wondering how he had wriggled past them in the space of a hall carpet. His goals were usually gems, passed rather than shot into the net.

Most of the first-team players back in those late Fifties used to either ignore us or play the big I am with we apprentices, but Jim was always friendly and never ever boastful or big-headed ... and he had much to boast about.

He has always been the best at everything he's done. He was even a world-class piss artist, then had the character to beat the bottle and become one of the most popular television performers in his double-act with The Saint, Ian St John. Now he has developed into one of the finest stand-up comedians in the business. If you don't believe me, catch one of his roadshows. He is guaranteed to have you pissing yourself.

Jim was already a legend by the time I arrived at the Bridge. It was part of Chelsea football folklore how he'd had his most prolific goalscoring season in 1956-57, while still an apprentice professional. He scored 114 goals and Chelsea presented him with an illuminated address to mark the feat. On the first day of the following season, he made his League debut and scored for Chelsea against Spurs at White Hart Lane. It was the start of the great goal rush.

I was choked for him when he missed out on the 1966 World Cup victory. Geoff Hurst was an outstanding striker, but would admit he was not fit to lace Jimmy's boots, or even his drinks.

Greavsie was out there on his own as a goalscorer. We were all disappointed at Chelsea when he chose to chase the lira and move to Italy. But it back-fired on Jim, because no sooner had he tied himself to Milan than the maximum wage in England was kicked out.

Suddenly he could earn as much in the First Division as in Italy, where he was as

Seventeen-year-old Jimmy Greaves on his way to the first of his 124 League goals for Chelsea against Spurs, which was a club record until Bobby Tambling came along.

miserable as sin and feeling like a prisoner in their then suffocating defensive game.

When it was obvious he was looking to come back home after just a handful of months we got excited at the Bridge because it was believed he was going to return to Chelsea. Our chairman Joe Mears went in with a big bid, but then stepped out of the picture when Spurs boss Bill Nicholson revealed he was ready to go to a mind-boggling hundred grand to take Jimmy to White Hart Lane.

In the end Bill Nick got him for £99,999, because he did not want Jim to be lumbered with the label of being the world's first £100,000 footballer. Today he would be worth nearer £59,999,999! It's little known that Bill Nick also fancied me, and he once asked me during an England Under-23 tour when he was manager if I would like to join Spurs. But I was and always will be Blue blooded.

Greavsie still has a big soft spot for Chelsea, and has told me he didn't want to return to the Bridge because he felt he had set standards there by which he would always be judged. And in signing for Tottenham, he was joining the Blanchflower-motivated team that had just become the first side of the 20th Century to win the League championship and FA Cup double.

He set all sorts of scoring records with Tottenham, helped them retain the FA Cup in 1962 and then become Britain's first winners of a major trophy when they captured the European Cup Winners' Cup in 1963.

I managed to keep the Artful Dodger quiet again in the 1967 FA Cup final when Spurs beat Chelsea 2-1 with goals from Jimmy Robertson and Frank Saul.

Jim wound down his career with a less-than-happy couple of seasons with West Ham, and then concentrated on his business career after retiring at the ridiculously young age of 31. He then went non-League, playing a leisurely deep-lying role with Brentwood, Chelmsford and Barnet ... overcame alcoholism, drove in the 1970 World Cup rally, conquered the world of television, became a newspaper columnist with *The Sun*, had loads of books published in harness with his big mate Norman Giller, and later took to the stage with enormous success under the guidance of our mutual pal Terry Baker.

The only thing Greavsie couldn't do was score goals against me. I get a kick out of saying that! Just don't tell him that I consider he's the top man.

QUOTE UNQUOTE: Jimmy Greaves

"I admit that I hated playing against Chopper. He was a nasty git, and followed me like a bad smell. But now, looking back on it all these years later, I have to hold my hands up and say he got the better of me. He deserved to win England recognition, but I don't think Alf had the bottle to pick him. He got enough stick over selecting Nobby Stiles. Chopper made Nobby seem about as hard as Graham Norton."

Born: Glasgow April 15 1940

Career span: 1958-74

**Clubs: East Stirling (1958-62)
Chelsea (1962-74)
331 League games, 1 goal**

Won 23 Scotland caps

**Chelsea honours: League Cup
winners' medal (1965), FA
Cup runners-up (1967), FA
Cup winners' medal (1970)**

EDDIE served Chelsea across the board for fifteen years, as player, coach and then manager. We had lots of laughs along the way, but it finally all ended in tears when he quit the club in a stupid argument over a motor car.

He was as good a left-back as I ever played with, lightning fast, good ball control and with a strong, decisive tackle that even I considered quite tasty,

As much as any full-back, he helped introduce the overlapping style of play that is now commonplace. You have to remember that Eddie and I grew up in an era when full-backs were tied totally to defence and were not encouraged or expected to cross over the halfway line.

The overlapping style was inroduced by the likes of Jimmy Armfield, Don Howe, George Cohen, Ray Wilson, Ken Shellito and our Eddie.

Yet for all his attacking play, he scored only five goals throughout his stay at Stamford Bridge. One of them will never be forgotten by those who witnessed it. The goal in a million came in the League Cup final home leg against Leicester. He picked the ball up deep in the Chelsea half and set off on an unbelievable run of eighty yards, beating a string of startled defenders who were expecting him to pass – as were his team-mates. He ended it by slipping the ball past the world's greatest goalkeeper, Gordon Banks. It was real Roy of the Rovers stuff, and helped us beat Leicester 3-2 on aggregate.

If Fulham had got their way, Eddie would have started his English career at Craven Cottage as successor to their long-serving left-back Jim Langley. But Tommy Doc, brought up in the same Glasgow area as Eddie, nipped in and brought him to the Bridge for a bargain five grand.

He won 23 Scotland caps, and played in the 1967 victory over England at Wembley when the Jocks cheekily claimed to be world champions after their 3-2 victory against nine fit England players. It was their first defeat since the 1966 World Cup triumph.

Not only did Eddie score that spectacular goal that virtually clinched the League Cup, but he played a big part in the winner against Leeds in the 1970 FA Cup final replay at Old Trafford. It was his persistence that won us the Ian Hutchinson throw-in from which David Webb headed the unforgettable winner in extra-time.

An injury cost Eddie the chance of playing in the European Cup Winners' Cup final the following season, and when he decided to hang up his boots he was given a job on the coaching staff.

Come April 1975 and Chelsea were in crisis, on their way to relegation and in enough debt to sink the Queen Mary. Eddie was appointed manager in succession to Ron Suart, and the first thing he did was take the captaincy away from me, thanks mate! Well, I guess I was creaking a bit. He handed it to the 18-year-old Butch Wilkins, and motivated a side mixed with young and old to instant promotion back from the Second Division.

Eddie believed, when negotiating his new contract for the start of the season,

that one of his perks should be a company car. Chairman Brian Mears disagreed, and Eddie quit on a matter of principle. He always was a stubborn sod – on and off the pitch. With hardly a backward glance, Eddie took himself off to the United States where he became manager of Memphis Rogues and, later, general manager of Cleveland.

He settled down to his all-American way of life and set up home in Knoxville, keeping his golf handicap down to single figures and staying in touch with the Premier League football via cable television. Nice one, steady Eddie.

QUOTE UNQUOTE: Eddie McCreadie

"I was proud of my achievements with Chelsea and Scotland. It was a pity it ended on a sour note, but nobody can take away from me the fifteen wonderful years I had at the Bridge. The highlights, of course, were the FA Cup in 1970 and I like to think my goal in the 1965 League Cup final was a little bit special. Getting the team back up to the First Division straightaway was as good as it gets as a manager, and I was very disappointed when the chairman could not meet what I thought was a reasonable request."

Born: East Ham April 18 1940

Career span: 1957-65

**Chelsea player (1957-65)
114 League games, 2 goals**

Chelsea coach (1966-77)

Chelsea manager (1977-78)

**Won 1 England Under-23 and
1 full cap in the 4-2 victory
over Czechoslovakia in 1963**

Qualified as FA Coach 1966

TO meet Ken Shellito you would never think he had been one of Chelsea's unluckiest players. He has always got a banana-size smile, and never moans about the crippling injury that ended his career just as he had reached his peak.

He was on Alf Ramsey's shortlist for the 1966 World Cup when a crocked knee forced him to hang up his boots at just 26. Ken is one of the few players I have allowed into my Top 50 list who played less than 150 matches for Chelsea. He and Eddie McCreadie were pioneers of overlapping play. George Cohen, who took his place in the England defence, is big enough to admit: "It's quite possible I wouldn't have made it into the England team in the 1966 World Cup final if Ken had not been injured. He was a superb player."

Despite the injury, Ken served Chelsea for nearly 25 years. He arrived at Stamford Bridge in 1955 on the very same day as his fellow East Londoner Jimmy Greaves. Both of them had been born in East Ham in 1940, and had been snapped up by Chelsea's famous scout Jimmy Thompson. "Ken was the most skilful and inventive right-back of his generation," Greavsie says. "But for his injury he would have won a shelf load of England caps."

By coincidence, Norman Giller – the writer helping me get my thoughts and comments down on paper – was born a mile down the road to Ken on exactly the same day, April 18 1940, so they always had a special bond. "Ken was as fast and skilful a right-back as I've ever seen and years ahead of his time," says Norm. "It was heartbreaking to watch the torture he went through with his knee problems."

Ken got his one England cap in Bobby Moore's first match as England captain, a 4-2 victory over Czechoslovakia in 1963. It was also the first England victory under the management of Alf Ramsey, who had been a magnificent right-back with Southampton and Tottenham. He battled and battled through several major operations to save his career, but finally had to concede he was not going to make it. Instead of moping and moaning, Ken switched all his energy to coaching and became a key man in the Chelsea backroom team. He set up the youth academy that produced a conveyor belt of outstanding players like Butch Wilkins and Clive Walker.

In 1977 he followed his old full-back partner Eddie McCreadie into the Chelsea hot seat and the highlight of his year in charge was a 4-2 FA Cup victory over the then European champions Liverpool and a place in the quarter-finals. But Ken was far too nice a guy to be a success as a manager, and we were back in the relegation mire when he made way for Danny Blanchflower in 1978.

What an adventure Ken's been on since leaving the Bridge. He coached at Queens Park Rangers, Crystal Palace and Preston before going to Texas to set up a Chelsea-style academy for the entire State. In 1987 he was lured back to a coaching and assistant manager role at Crystal Palace and then had a spell as youth team organiser at Coventry.

Next stop was Malaysia, where our Ken has become a legend. He has coached several teams to the local championships, and has his own academy in the beautiful setting of Kota Kinabalu, where he's set up home and is so settled he has become a Malaysian 'Permanent Resident' and has a beautiful Malaysian wife. It's a long long way from Kings Road.

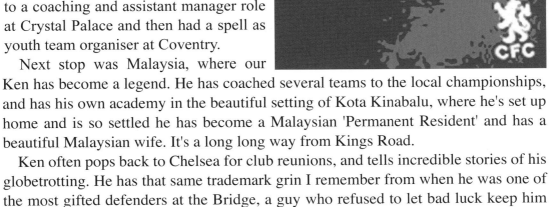

Ken often pops back to Chelsea for club reunions, and tells incredible stories of his globetrotting. He has that same trademark grin I remember from when he was one of the most gifted defenders at the Bridge, a guy who refused to let bad luck keep him down. He's a great example of what can be achieved with hard work and dedication.

QUOTE UNQUOTE: Ken Shellito

"Once I knew my playing days were over, I threw myself into studying every aspect of coaching and was lucky to have the influence of people like Tommy Doc and Dave Sexton. My injury was a freak thing. I did not have the satisfaction of being kicked up in the air by somebody like Chopper. I caught my studs in the Stamford Bridge turf, turned and wrecked my knee. I was supposed to have been playing for England against the Rest of the World the following week. Oh well, that's life ..."

Born: Norwich April 29 1941

Career span: 1958-74

**Clubs: Chelsea (1958-66)
176 League games, 80 goals
Birmingham City (1966-68),
QPR (1968-70), Millwall
(1970-72), Brighton & Hove
Albion (1972-74)
Total League goals: 189**

Won 4 England caps, 1 goal

**Chelsea honours: League Cup
winner (1965)**

I OFTEN wonder how the career of Barry Bridges might have gone if he had not been involved in the Blackpool Affair. For those of you not around at the time, Tommy Docherty sensationally sent home eight players from the seaside resort for partying when they should have been sleeping.

We had been in with an outside chance of winning the First Division title in April 1965 when the Doc exploded with anger during a training trip to Blackpool ahead of a match against Burnely at Turf Moor.

Eight players had gone against his orders and joined in a party in the town. The next day the Doc sent them all home and brought in a load of reserves to take their place at Burnley, where we got stuffed 6-2!

Barry was one of the players, along with Terry Venables, George Graham, Eddie McCreadie, John Hollins, Joe Fascione, Bert Murray and Marvin Hinton. I was never a party animal, so there was no chance of me being one of them. That's not me being a goody two-shoes. I preferred my kip to a party.

Barry took the Doc's medicine harder than most, and from then on he and the manager hardly had a civil word for each other. You could say the bridges were broken between them. Barry always argued that Docherty should have hit the players with a heavy fine and kept it all out of the newspapers. But from the moment he sent them home, the media had a free-for-all and for days it was a hot topic on the front as well as back pages, and the heavy defeat by Burnley kept the story running.

It all came when Barry was in the hottest form of his career. He had been a key player in helping us get straight back up from the Second Division, and in the season of the Blackpool Affair he was top League scorer with 27 goals, had helped us lift the League Cup and there was a time when both the League title and FA Cup were in our sights. Barry was one of the quickest forwards in the League, equally happy on the wing or leading the attack. Feeding off the passes of Terry Venables, he and Bobby Tambling were electric together. I would have hated to try to defend against them when the pair of them were really motoring.

But a lot of the drive went out of Barry after the Blackpool business, and it was no great surprise when he was sold on to Birmingham in May 1966 for a then club record £55,000. After winning four England caps, he was in Alf Ramsey's 40-man squad for the World Cup, but did not make the final 22-man cut.

He banged in 37 League goals for the other Blues – Birmingham – before becoming a busy have-boots-will-travel player – finding the net for Queens Park Rangers, Millwall and Brighton.

Barry then moved to Highlands Park in South Africa, found himself a new wife, Megan, and later became player-manager in Ireland with St Patrick's Athletic and Sligo Rovers before returning to his home County of Norfolk to manage Dereham Town and, finally, Horsford United.

Never one to duck a challenge, Barry took over the running of his grandfather's dairy farm in Norfolk and did the daily milk round before switching to a completely new life as a newsagent. He and Megan ran the business together for more than twenty years before retiring a couple of years ago to concentrate on continuing to provide respite care for children with special needs.

He has been to several Chelsea reunions and always receives a hero's welcome back home to the club where his career started in the Drake Ducklings era more than 50 years ago.

Yes, just what would have happened to his Chelsea and England career but for that Blackpool Affair and the volcanic fall-out with Tommy Docherty?

QUOTE UNQUOTE: Barry Bridges

"It's hardly a secret that I fell out with Tommy Docherty over the way he handled the Blackpool incident. Anyway, that's all in the mists of time. I loved my days at the Bridge, and was proud of my achievements. I have never got Chelsea out of my blood. Once a Chelsea player always a Chelsea player. That team with Catty, Eddie McCreadie, Lou Hinton, Venners, George Graham, John Hollins, Bobby Tambling – and Chopper, of course – took some beating ..."

BOBBY'S phenomenal, all-time goalscoring record for Chelsea deserves special projection ...

Born Storrington, Sussex, September 18 1941

Career span: 1958-73

Internationl honours: England schools, 13 England Under-23 caps, 3 full caps, 1 goal

202 goals in total for Chelsea, a club record

164 League goals for Chelsea, a club record

25 FA Cup goals for Chelsea, a club record

10 League Cup goals and **3** in Europe

5 goals in one First Division match for Chelsea against Aston Villa in a 6-2 victory at Villa Park on September 17 1966

A League Cup winner with Chelsea in 1965, he scored the consolation goal in the 1967 FA Cup final 2-1 defeat by Tottenham (this was the first goal scored by a Chelsea player in an FA Cup final).

12 goals for Crystal Palace

Helped Cork Celtic win the League of Ireland championship; represented the League of Ireland against Argentina in 1978 while with Waterford; played for Shamrock Rovers and Cork Alberts; and has managed Irish clubs Cork Celtic, Cork City and Crosshaven.

BOBBY had the impossible task of following in the goalscoring footsteps of Jimmy Greaves, and he did the job so well that he took over from Greavsie as the all-time record marksman for Chelsea.

The only disappointing thing for Bobby is that he did not have a cupboard-full of medals to show for his incredible scoring feats. He had to make do with just the Football League trophy award in 1965 that, in those days, was a tankard rather than a medal. We beat Leicester in the two-leg final just a couple of years before it became a one-off with a Wembley setting. Bobby scored in our 3-2 victory at the Bridge, followed by a goalless draw at Filbert Street. There was also an FA Cup runners-up medal, when he snatched our only goal in the 2-1 defeat by Tottenham in the 1967 final. Amazingly, this was the first goal ever netted by a Chelsea player in an FA Cup final.

So if you measure Bobby's career by the trophies he won, it was not very noteworthy. But measure it by the goals he scored and he was up there with the giants of the game.

Chelsea had nicked Bobby from under the noses of Portsmouth. He played his youth soccer at Hayling Island, and Fratton Park seemed the obvious place for him to start his career, but legendary scout Jimmy Thompson nipped in and took him to the Bridge to join Drake's Ducklings.

He was pitched into the first-team at the age of just seventeen, poaching the winning goal in a dramatic 3-2 victory over West Ham. He remembers that at the time he was earning – wait for it – £10 a week! Once he was eighteen, he was paid the maximum wage of twenty quid. These were the crazy days when a player down in the Fourth (or Third Division South) Division was earning exactly the same £20-a-week as the likes of Stanley Matthews and Tom Finney in the First Division.

There was a smell of revolution in the air when Bobby and I first came into the first-team squad, and I remember us being balloted for strike action in the 1960-61 season. Suddenly, under verbal attack from Jimmy Hill and the PFA (the players' union) the bosses gave in and kicked out the maximum wage.

When Greavsie left for Milan – just as Johnny Haynes down the road at Fulham was made the first £100-a-week footballer – the responsibility of being the main striker fell to Bobby, and he responded by banging in goals galore. He and Barry Bridges struck up a prolific partnership, with Terry Venables and tiny Tommy Harmer feeding them with passes from midfield.

He found the net an incredible 35 times in the 1962-63 season, when we scrambled our way straight back to the First Division, with Bobby as our captain as well as our top scorer. Tommy Docherty had taken over from Ted Drake as manager, and we were really bombing after the disappointment of relegation.

When Barry moved on to Birmingham, Bobby then forged a great understanding with the young Peter Osgood, and I am sure we would have won some silverware in those mid-sixties but for Ossie breaking a leg just as we were looking as good an attacking side as any in the League.

Greavsie's famous description of Frank Blunstone having a heart the size of a cabbage could have also been used to sum up Bobby. He would run for the team until the cows came home, had electrifying pace and a potent left foot finish. I remember him once thumping in five goals in a First Division match against Aston Villa at Villa Park. We won 6-2 and Bobby might easily have had ten goals that day. He was really on fire.

Along with the rest of us, he suffered the heartbreak of two successive FA Cup semi-final defeats before we managed to reach the final against Spurs, when he had the consolation of scoring our one goal.

Bobby became the victim of a run of injuries so, by the time the Dave Sexton era started, he was spending more time in the treatment room than at the training ground. One of Chelsea's greatest servants sadly missed out on the golden days of the Cup successes. He moved on to Crystal Palace, where he was a yard short of the pace that had made him such a feared finisher at the Bridge.

Like a thoroughbred racehorse, Bobby could operate properly only on soft going. Hard pitches made his life a misery.

Paddy Mulligan, a great Irish character who had a spell at Chelsea, told him that he should go to Ireland to play because the pitches were generally softer over there.

At first, Paddy had meant it as a joke but it soon dawned on both of them that it made sense, and it was Paddy who was the go-between for Bobby to start a new phase of his career in Ireland.

He became something of a legend with a cluster of clubs, including playing for the League of Ireland against Argentina in 1978, the year they won the World Cup in Buenos Aires.

Bobby later settled down to manage and live full time in his adopted home of Cork. He is always a very welcome guest at the Bridge, where there is a hospitality room named in his honour. His goals will always carry the message to Stamford Bridge fans right down the years: "Bobby Tambling Was Here."

QUOTE UNQUOTE: Bobby Tambling

"I wouldn't swap my years at the Bridge for anything. They were smashing days, but they would have been even better if we had not lost the back-to-back FA Cup semi-finals against Liverpool and Sheffield Wednesday. I just wish Tommy Docherty had not lost his patience after the defeat by Wednesday. I am sure if he had kept the team together we would have won one of the major trophies. But as I look back I have only good memories, and I've been lucky to find a happy life in Ireland."

Bobby Tambling strikes with his potent left foot that scored goals galore for Chelsea

Born: Putney September 27 1941
Career span: 1960-79

Chelsea (1960-79)
600 League games

Also played briefly for St Louis Stars, Dundee United and Woking in the Isthmian League.

England caps: 7

Chelsea honours: League Cup (1965), FA Cup (1970), European Cup Winners' Cup (1971)

IN all my years playing and watching football, I have not seen a better catcher of the ball than Catty Bonetti. He would fly through the air like Superman and clutch the ball out of thin air in situations where most goalies would have been trying to punch it clear or missing it all together.

He was, in my opinion, as good a goalkeeper as Chelsea have ever had, and he was a challenger for my club appearances record with 600 League games. Peter arrived at the club in strange circumstances, and for once it was not scout Jimmy Thompson who spotted him. Taking the credit was his Mum!

She wrote to manager Ted Drake recommending him after he had played for Worthing and Brighton schools. The family, with a Swiss background, had settled in Worthing, where they ran a seaside café.

He was given a trial and was, of course snapped up, and made his debut at the age of 18 in 1959 with a First Division victory over Manchester City. Peter quickly earned the nickname The Cat, with his lightning reflexes and graceful diving. He always managed to be elegant between the posts, no matter how great the pressure, and was a brilliant one-arm thrower of the ball.

Like many of the players, he had his ups-and-downs with the controversial Tommy Docherty, and was on the point of demanding a transfer when the Doc amazingly signed Alex Stepney from Millwall in 1966. The rumour was that Tommy was going to play Stepney and Bonetti in alternate matches, but then Matt Busby came in to take Stepney to Old Trafford and Peter settled down to give the club great loyal service.

Catty won seven England caps, and it would have been many more but for the presence of Gordon Banks and then Peter Shilton and Ray Clemence. Those were the days when we had the best goalkeepers in the world.

I felt sorry for Peter when he carried the can for England's 3-2 defeat by West Germany in the 1970 World Cup quarter-final in Mexico, losing a 2-0 lead. Catty had been called into the team at the last minute because Gordon Banks became ill, and he looked responsible for two of the German goals. But in Peter's defence it should be pointed out that this was his first full competitive match since the end of the previous season when he had played a major part in our FA Cup final replay victory over Leeds at Old Trafford.

Suddenly he was pitched into a match at high altitude with a ball that played all sorts of tricks in the thin air. It was understandable that he failed to reach the high standards he had set in England.

The Cat was big enough to shrug off the heavy criticism aimed at him by know-all critics, and the following season played an important part in our European Cup Winners' Cup victory over Real Madrid in Athens.

Peter left Chelsea on a free transfer in 1975 and had a successful year with St Louis Stars in the North American Soccer League, but returned to the Bridge at the request of Eddie McCreadie. He helped the young Chelsea team gain promotion back to the First Division in 1976-77, and played his final match in May 1979 in a 1-1 draw with Arsenal. It was his 729th competitive game for the club, and I'm proud to say that only I have bettered that fantastic figure. He kept more than 200 clean sheets and was always thoroughly professional and committed to doing his best for the team.

His adventures since have included being a postman on the Isle of Mull, playing briefly for Dundee United, and coaching with Chelsea, Manchester City and England – picking up his World Cup medal in 2009 for being a member of the triumphant 1966 squad.

The Cat had got the cream.

QUOTE UNQUOTE: Peter Bonetti

"Probably the most memorable of all the matches I played for Chelsea was the FA Cup final replay against Leeds at Old Trafford. It was certainly one of my most painful games. I got clobbered by Mick Jones early on and had an aching knee that these days would have meant a straight substitution. But back then you didn't have goalkeepers on the bench. It has been called the roughest match ever played, but we battled through it and no victory ever tasted sweeter against our deadly rivals from Elland Road."

Born Fife: October 14 1942
Career span: 1961-78

Played for Aberdeen and
Dundee before signing for
Chelsea (1966-72/1974-78)
299 League games, 22 goals
Crystal Palace (1972-74)
44 League games

Scotland caps: 16

Chelsea honours: FA Cup
runners-up (1967), winner
(1970), European Cup
Winners' Cup (1971)

BONNY Prince Charlie joined us from Dundee in 1966, allowing Tommy Docherty to ship out Terry Venables to Tottenham. From his first League match – when he ran rings round the great Bobby Moore – Charlie was a huge favourite with the Stamford Bridge fans.

While he was replacing Venners, Charlie was a totally different player. Terry liked to direct things from midfield, setting up attacks with long, well-directed passes. Charlie on the other hand was content to drift in and out of games, and when he was in possession he liked to go on long dribbling runs, beating defenders with old-style winger tricks.

Nobody who saw the FA Cup final replay victory at Old Trafford over Leeds will forget Charlie's dazzling run before setting up Peter Osgood for the first goal that knocked the wind out of Leeds. It was a moment of sheer genius.

I've rarely known a player who could control a ball as well as Charlie. He was as clever as a circus juggler. Sometimes the ball would seem to be tied to his boots as if on an invisible string, and defenders would be left kicking thin air. But he could also be frustrating by holding on to the ball too long, or going back to beat a defender he had already roasted. The surprising thing is he did not score more goals, and if he had been a better finisher he would have won many more than his sixteen Scotland caps.

We were all shocked when Charlie was allowed to move to Crystal Palace in 1972, but he returned eighteen months later and helped Eddie McCreadie's young side gain promotion. He later emigrated to the United States, playing for several clubs out there before starting a successful coaching school in Ohio. On his trips back to London he finds he has lost none of his popularity at the Bridge.

QUOTE UNQUOTE: Charlie Cooke

"They were fun and often mad days at Chelsea. We played hard on and off the pitch. Nothing was ever predictable. Since coming here to the States I have got great satisfaction passing on the things I have learned to youngsters keen to master a game that is growing in popularity every minute."

Born: Dagenham, January 6 1943
Career span: 1960-76

Clubs: Chelsea (1960-66) 202 League games, 26 goals Tottenham Hotspur (1966-69), QPR (1969-74), Crystal Palace (1974-76)

Chelsea honours: League Cup (1965)

Only player capped at every level by England: schools, youth, amateur, Under-23 and 2 full caps

Manager: Crystal Palace, QPR, Barcelona, Tottenham Hotspur, England, Australia, Middlesbrough, Leeds

IT is no secret that Terry Venables and I were never bosom buddies in our young days. We had no problems playing with each other and I like to think I balanced Venners nicely, winning the ball and then giving it to him to do the creative stuff.

But I just did not like the bloke, and I know the feeling was mutual. For me he was too flash and full of himself. If he'd been a bar of chocolate he would have eaten himself.

Tommy Docherty didn't like him most of the time either, and I remember when he sold him to Tottenham he said: "There can only be one manager of Chelsea ... and it's not going to be Venables."

Putting personal feelings aside, I accept that he could pass the ball better than most and had a sharp footballing brain. If he had been as good as he thought he was he would have been Cruyff and di Stefano rolled into one. He played with a swagger, and had good control of the ball but couldn't tackle his way out of a paper bag. He had a unique full house of England caps at every level, but only two full ones – mind you, that was two more than me.

All Chelsea had to show under his midfield leadership was two losing FA Cup semi-finals and a League Cup victory in 1965. He won an FA Cup winners' medal against us with Spurs in 1967, but as I understand it was never very popular at White Hart Lane, and he later played for QPR and Crystal Palace without setting the world alight.

He got a great media image thanks to Fleet Street people like Norman Giller and Jeff Powell sucking up to him. His managerial career took in stops at Crystal Palace, QPR, and Barcelona – where he became known as El Tel after they had won La Liga. He then returned to England to not only manage Spurs but also become owner, until falling out with Alan Sugar, the man who had put up most of the money.

El Tel was rarely out of the headlines, often for the wrong reasons. He got involved in some dodgy business deals that were well-documented, but this did not stop him becoming England manager for what was a relatively successful spell.

Then his soccer travels took him to Australia, Portsmouth (as chairman), back to Crystal Palace and then up to Middlesbrough and Leeds. He was a television pundit for BBC and then ITV, apparently wrote loads of books and was briefly England assistant manager under Steve McClaren, when England were arguably at their worst.

He had a London drinking club called Scribes; co-devised a board game called The Manager; co-created a television character called Hazell; has had newspaper columns in the *News of the World* and *The Sun;* half-a-dozen other business interests and has been in the charts with some so-so singing records. When he was at Chelsea he used to sing at Hamersmith Palais with the Joe Loss band. The Doc said he was a dead loss!

Terry and I are on fairly good terms these days, but we are not on each other's Christmas card list. He has had a full and varied life – a real busy bollocks – and good luck to him as he approaches his 70s. He is just not my cup of tea. And I'm sure he couldn't care less.

QUOTE UNQUOTE: Terry Venables

"There were times at Chelsea in the early Sixties when we played some magnificent football, but we had a manager who always wanted to fix things when they weren't broke. I liked to play football that was constructive. Others didn't."

Born: Gateshead, June 10 1945
Career span: 1962-1978

Clubs: Arsenal (1962-66)
Chelsea (1966-74)
187 League games, 74 goals
Millwall (loan 1974)
Manchester United (loan 1974) Brentford (1977-78)
Total League games: 232, 87 goals

2 England Under-23 caps

Chelsea honours: FA Cup (1970), European Cup Winners' Cup (1971)

TOMMY arrived at the Bridge as the makeweight in the transfer in 1966 that took George Graham to Arsenal, as Tommy Doc went through his rebuilding process after deciding to break up the team that had only been good enough to reach two successive FA Cup semi-finals.

Many people thought we had got ourselves a Highbury reject, when in fact Tommy proved himself a very useful addition to the side. He was an energetic and enthusiastic support player, taking the pressure off the young, inexperienced Peter Osgood with his decoy runs. Tommy also knew the way to goal himself, and banged in lots of vital goals.

Tommy was also a welcome member of the Chelsea drinking club, and he got in quite a few scrapes with his party pals Ossie, Alan Hudson and Charlie Cooke. He was a handsome guy and it got a lot of publicity at the time when he walked off with the wife of Michael Crawford, actor and Chelsea supporter. Yes, he was quite a character in a team of big personalities.

We nicknamed Tommy 'Sponge' and told the Fleet Street boys that this was because of the way he soaked up the work on the pitch. In fact, it was because of the way he soaked up the booze. He had hollow legs.

He had a loan spell at Millwall, and also played two matches for Manchester United when Tommy Doc brought him in during an injury crisis at Old Trafford. Then he had a wind-down season at Brentford, played for Gravesend and then in Seattle and coached at Griffin Park. These days he pops up in pub quizzes: "Name the two Chelsea players who have also appeared for Manchester United and Arsenal." The answer: Tommy and George Graham.

QUOTE UNQUOTE: Tommy Baldwin

"The players don't seem to be having the same sort of fun now. We used to go to the local boozer after games and see the supporters. They would tell you if you'd had a good game or not. Nowadays they go their own way after matches. There's not the same camaraderie."

Born: Battersea, December 24 1945

Died: March 20 1977

Career span: 1962-77

Clubs: Chelsea (1960-75) 269 League games, 20 goals Oxford United (1975-77) 65 League games, 2 goals

Chelsea honours: FA Cup (1970), European Cup Winners' Cup (1971)

I CAN'T think of Peter Houseman without filling up. He was tragically killed along with his wife and two close friends in a car smash in Oxford in 1977, and everybody whose path he crossed still deeply feels the loss.

He was not only a fine footballer, but also a lovely modest man, quiet and respectful. Peter did not have a boastful bone in his body, and so would never have claimed to be the person most responsible for our FA Cup success of 1970.

Anybody who watched all our matches on the way to the final against Leeds will know that I am not exaggerating when I say that it was Peter who dragged us back into the running for the trophy when all seemed lost.

Peter was a local boy made good, born just across the Thames from the Bridge at Battersea. He came up through the juniors, and took quite a while to establish himself. But Dave Sexton recognised that he had gifts that perhaps Tommy Docherty had not uncovered. Whether playing at full-back, in midfield or out on the left-wing, Peter proved that he was the perfect team player, fetching and carrying the ball and creating chances galore for our strikers. Peter Osgood and Ian Hutchinson, in particular, were grateful to feed off him. He was a players' player, not always appreciated by the fans but whose quiet work was vital to the team performance.

The game that sticks out most in my memory is the fourth round FA Cup replay at Turf Moor after Burnley had held us to a draw at the Bridge. Just over fifteen minutes to go, and we were trailing 1-0 and looking on the way out. Then Peter collected the ball deep in our half and set off on a run that took him ghosting past three Burnley challenges before he smashed an unstoppable shot into the Burnley net for an equaliser that forced extra-time. He then provided the pass for Tommy Baldwin to put us ahead in extra-time and finished off his man-of-the-match performance with a third goal to finally bury Burnley.

He played just as vital a role in the semi-final against Watford. It was his cross that created the chance for Ossie to give us a 2-1 led, and he scored twice himself in the 5-1 win. Peter was an ever-present in the team that season, and it was his 25 yard shot that gave us our first equaliser against Leeds in the final on the mudheap of a pitch that was Wembley.

He was just as influential the following season as he helped us win the European Cup Winners' Cup with a string of outstanding performances.

Peter was never a flamboyant type of player, so his best work often went unnoticed expect by his team-mates. We all knew that it was his energy, enthusiasm and delicate touch on the ball that was making the team tick.

It was amazing the number of times we analysed goals to find out that Peter had played a part. In these days of statisticians noting assists, he would have been a regular on the report sheet.

We felt we were losing a member of our family when he moved on in 1975, joining Oxford United after playing nearly 350 games for us and scoring 39 goals.

It was a terrible shock when we heard of his death in an accident on the A40 on a return journey from a fund-raising event. He was just thirty-two. We were only too happy and eager to play in a series of benefit matches to raise money for the children orphaned by the terrible crash.

Peter's name lives on in a youth league named after him in Oakley in Hampshire, a village where he voluntarily used to coach a local youth football team.

That was typical of Peter, always quietly helping out others. It was a pleasure knowing and playing with him.

QUOTE UNQUOTE: Peter Houseman

After the 1970 FA Cup semi-final victory over Watford:
"This is something I have dreamed about since I was a boy growing up in Battersea ... playing for Chelsea in an FA Cup final at Wembley. We will start underdogs against Leeds because they have so many international-quality players, but I am confident we will rise to the occasion and give them a real battle. I don't think it will be a game for the faint-hearted!"

Born: Hampstead, March 15 1946

Career span: 1964-75

Clubs: Fulham (1964-69) 149 League games, 4 goals Chelsea (1969-75) 165 League games, 4 goals

Republic of Ireland caps: 19, 1 goal

Chelsea honours: FA Cup (1970), European Cup Winners' Cup (1971)

John's arrival from Fulham in the New Year of 1969 gave us the stability and authority we had been missing in the middle of our defence. We were a tight-knit bunch, but John had a pleasant personality and quickly fitted in.

In his first full season he picked up an FA Cup winners' medal and the following season we won the European Cup Winners' Cup. It was no coincidence that these major trophies arrived along with John.

We used to tease London-born John that he only got his 19 Irish caps because he had once smelled an Irish barmaid's apron, but if he had not taken up his invitation to play for Ireland he would have been challenging for a place in the England defence.

He was a hard and powerful centre-half, who always tried to play the ball out of defence instead of just lumping it. John quickly got an important understanding with our goalkeeper Peter Bonetti, and this was a major reason for Chelsea's sudden tightening at the back after too many seasons leaking goals that stopped us winning the big prizes. For a player who often went into the opposition penalty area it was a surprise that he scored only five goals for Chelsea, but one of them just happened to be the goal that won us the Cup Winners' Cup in Athens.

An even bigger surprise from John was the direction his life took after he finished playing. He had a year in Philadelphia with Peter Osgood as a team-mate for the Fury, winning the NASL Defender of the Year title, with a certain Franz Beckenbauer in second place. After briefly managing Dundalk, Maidenhead and Egham Town he switched to a new, rewarding world of care work, specialising in helping adults with autism and learning difficulties. John has really given something back to the community, and makes me feel very humble.

QUOTE UNQUOTE: John Dempsey

"I can honestly say my care work has given me as much satisfaction as my footballing career. It's a completely different world, of course, and I have had to show the sort of patience that would have been out of place on the pitch. I loved my stay at Chelsea, and have many great memories."

Art Turner
2010

Born: Stratford, London. April 9 1946
Career span: 1963-1984

Clubs: Leyton Orient (1963-65) Southampton (1965-68) Chelsea (1968-74)
230 League games, 21 goals
QPR (1974-77) Leicester (1977-78) Derby (1978-80) Bournemouth (1980-83) Torquay (1983-84)
Total League games: 555, 35 goals

Chelsea honours: FA Cup (1970), European Cup Winners' Cup (1971)

Manager: Bournemouth, Torquay, Southend, Chelsea, Brentford, Yeovil

WEBBIE will always be part of Chelsea folklore because of the dramatic winning goal he scored against Leeds in the never-to-be-forgotten 1970 FA Cup final replay. He won lots of fans for the way he recovered from a nightmare game in the first match at Wembley.

Eddie Gray, the ball-playing Leeds winger, gave him a terrible roasting, which would have made many players want to run away and hide in embarrassment. But Webbie, of the Desperate Dan looks, was made of granite and had the character to play brilliantly in the replay at Old Trafford.

Dave Sexton spared him another chasing by Gray, and switched him to the middle of the defence alongside John Dempsey, with me given the brief of keeping Mr Gray under lock and key. Job done.

Webbie had been brought to Stamford Bridge by Dave Sexton, who was always his number one fan. He had him as a kid at Orient, and knew that while he was not the most skilful of players he had a huge heart and a fierce competitive spirit.

Brought up in a house in the same road as the Leyton Orient stadium, David at first had his sights on starting his career with West Ham. But they let him go before he had turned professional and it was under Dave Sexton at Orient that he first started making a name for himself. Dave signed Webbie for a third time when he took him to Queens Park Rangers in 1974, and he teamed-up with Frank McLintock in the middle of an impressive defence in the season that QPR finished their best ever second in the old First Division table.

A Del Boy of a character, Webbie later travelled the football circuit as a player with Leicester City, Derby County, Bournemouth and Torquay before starting a managerial career with Bournemouth, then Torquay and Southend. He was put in temporary charge at Chelsea as successor to Ian Porterfield in the days when the manager's office at the Bridge was fitted with a revolving door. Dave did a great job in keeping Chelsea up, but was not rewarded with the permanent job, losing out to Glenn Hoddle.

Never one to be lazy, Webbie got back on his bike and managed Brentford and Yeovil before taking a consultancy role back at Southend. He spends as much time as he can with his wife in the Cayman Islands, which is where he says he would like to one day settle down, but you can bet your boots that he would find a football club out there to manage!

Of all the clubs with which he has been associated, it is Chelsea where he has left his lasting mark and he will always be able to say: "I was the man who scored the goal that first won the FA Cup for the Blues."

QUOTE UNQUOTE: David Webb

"I was the whipping boy at Wembley where Eddie Gray gave me the mummy and daddy of a chasing. My confidence was at an all-time low at the end of the match but I remember the actor Michael Crawford patting me on the back and saying how much he admired my guts for sticking to my job. That pepped me up, and Dave Sexton made a winning tactical switch by putting me in the middle of the defence for the replay with the one and only Chopper putting the fear of God into Gray. Scoring the winning goal was the greatest moment of my career."

Born: Guildford, July 16 1946
Career span: 1963-1984

Clubs: Chelsea (1963-75)
436 League games, 47 goals
QPR (1975-79) Arsenal (1979-83) Chelsea (1983-84)
29 League games, 1 goal
Total League games: 743, 63 goals

Chelsea honours: FA Cup (1970), Cup Winners' Cup (1971), League Cup (1965), FA Cup (1967 runners-up)

England caps: 1

Manager: Chelsea, QPR (caretaker), Swansea, Rochdale, Stockport (caretaker)

JOHN was Mr Energy and played a prominent part in all our Cup successes of that golden period in the 1970s, but he was unlucky that injury kept him out of the Cup Winners' Cup replay in Athens. He ran his socks off for Chelsea in two playing periods at the Bridge, and later briefly served the club as manager.

If anybody was born to play football it was Olly. His father, grandfather and three brothers were all professional footballers. He deserved more than the one England cap he won, while his goalkeeping brother Dave was capped by Wales eleven times.

John and I dovetailed perfectly. While I was content to win the ball and then give it to a team-mate better positioned or better equipped to use it, John would motor up and down the pitch at a great rate of knots.While I rarely crossed into the opposition half, he often set up camp there, serving the forwards and sometimes striking important goals himself with a strong right-foot shot. It was as if he had an extra pair of lungs, and you could count his bad games on the fingers of a one-armed bandit.

Because he was so consistent and reliable, the Chelsea fans twice voted him their Player of the Year. He was also voted Player of the Year at QPR and Arsenal.

His most prolific season was 1971-72 when he helped himself to seventeen goals. That was the season we reached the League Cup final, going down to Stoke City and George Eastham at Wembley. It was after that match that our team gradually started to break up as the club got into a financial mess.

In between his two playing spells at Chelsea, John – along wth David Webb – followed Dave Sexton to Queens Park Rangers, and then he had three seasons with Arsenal. While at Highbury he was honoured with an MBE.

He returned to the Bridge in 1983 during the John Neal era, helping them win promotion back to the First Division in 1983-84 while playing a purely defensive role. He hung up his boots at the end of that season after a marathon run of 939 matches in total.

A year later John joined the queue of ex-Chelsea players who had a shot at the manager's job. After a great start during which Chelsea had a short period at the top of the First Division, John and his assistant Ernie Walley ran into what can be best described as player power. They fell out with key team members, in particular David Speedie and Nigel Spackman. It all came apart and John was sacked in March 1988 after a run of four months without a League win.

He has since tried his hand at the sports promotions agency lark, and has travelled the mangerial roundabout with QPR, Swansea, Rochdale and Stockport. His oddest job was taking charge of Stockport Tigers, the Chinese affiliate club of Stockport County. He found some of the players living in the dressing-room, and too undernourished to train properly!

Among his aggravating experiences have been being sacked by fax during contract negotiations with Rochdale, and falling out with Nicolas Anelka's brother, Claude, and resigning when assistant manager to him at Raith Rovers. He has also managed outside the Football League with Crawley Town and Weymouth, and was a member of the BBC Five Live radio team. His most successful season as a manager was 1999-2000, when he steered Swansea City to promotion as Third Division champions. His main claim to fame these days is that he is the father of Strictly Come Dancing winner Chris Hollins, BBCtv sports newsman who is a dead ringer for his Dad.

QUOTE UNQUOTE: John Hollins

"My happiest days in football were at Chelsea in the early 1970s. We not only had an exceptional team but also a wonderful team spirit, with lots of good banter in the dressing-room. The way some players behaved when I became manager, they would not have lasted five minutes under Tommy Doc or Dave Sexton. There was a total lack of respect. For those of my generation, the revolution at Chelsea has been just unbelievable. I never thought I would see the day when the club would be awash with money."

Born: Motherwell, December 25 1946

Career span: 1964-1974

Clubs: Chelsea (1964-73) 198 League games, 10 goals Brighton (1973) Leyton Orient (1973-74) Total League games: 226, 10 goals

Chelsea honours: League Cup (1965), European Cup Winners' Cup (1971), FA Cup (1967 runners-up)

I ONCE saw John Boyle described as the gentle man's Chopper Harris. John was much too nice a guy to be as nasty as me, but Tommy Docherty did his best to turn him into a destroyer rather than a creator. He used to say that I tackled with a chopper, and he wanted John to use a claymore.

Yes, it was a different game back in those days. A man's game. A game of physical contact.

When John and I were playing in tandem it took a brave forward to get past one of us, and a bloody mad one to try to take us both on.

John, born on Christmas Day, was a quiet, shy boy when he arrived at the Bridge as a fifteen-year-old schoolboy asking for a trial while on holiday from Motherwell. He brought with him a pair of football boots, passed his trial with flying colours and was taken on as an apprentice professional.

By the time he was eighteen he was a member of the first-team squad, and made his debut in the League Cup semi-final against Aston Villa, and a few weeks later picked up a winners' tankard as part of our side that beat Leicester City 3-2 in the two-legged final.

He was involved in all our Cup successes of the following few years apart from the FA Cup final when he was out injured, and was encouraged by Dave Sexton to add attacking skills to his powerful defensive technique.

John later moved on to Brighton and then Leyton Orient before becoming player-coach of Tampa Bay Rowdies, teaming up with Rodney Marsh and Eddie Firmani.

On his return to the UK he settled down in Kent, and worked for a security firm in London.

QUOTE UNQUOTE: John Boyle

"Playing in that Chelsea team was an absolute dream. We had a great mix of skill, speed and steel. Myself, Chopper, John Dempsey, Webbie and Hutch would look after the physical side; and with players like Ossie, Hud and Cookie we were always good on the eye. Happy days."

LET'S kick-off the Peter Osgood Chelsea story with his phenomenal goalscoring collection ...

Born Windsor, Berkshire, February 20 1947. Died: March 1 2006
Career span: 1964-79
Internationl honours: England Youth, 6 England Under-23 caps, 4 full caps.
Wore the No. 20 England shirt at the 1970 World Cup in Mexico

150 goals in total for Chelsea

105 League goals for Chelsea

19 FA Cup goals for Chelsea

16 Goals in Europe and **10 League Cup goals**

8 goals in the historic 1969-70 FA Cup triumph, including Chelsea's first goal in the final replay against Leeds at Old Trafford. The last player to score in every round of an FA Cup campaign.

5 goals in Chelsea's Cup record 13-0 victory over Jeunesse Hautcharage in the European Cup Winners' Cup first round second-leg tie at Stamford Bridge on September 29 1971. Scored in the 1971 European Cup Winners' Cup final against Real Madrid and netted Chelsea's Cup-clinching goal in the replay. Chelsea's leading League marksman in 1967-68, 1969-70, 1971-72, 1972-73

28 goals for Southampton and an FA Cup winners' medal in 1976.

THERE have been players who have scored more goals and made more appearances for Chelsea than Peter Osgood, and there have been players who have worked harder on the pitch, and players who have been more disciplined and dedicated ... but none of them can get within a mile of rivalling Ossie as the King of Stamford Bridge.

As well as being the most naturally gifted footballer I ever played with, Ossie was a lovable rascal whose behaviour was sometimes questionable. But for all his faults and foolishness, you could not help but like the guy. In fact many of us loved him, and that is why his legend will last as long as football is played at the Bridge.

It was typical of Ossie that he made headlines with his death. He died of a heart attack at the age of 59 while attending a family funeral in the spring of 2006, and it plunged all of us who knew him well into mourning his loss yet celebrating having been part of his life and football career. He was a real one-off.

Peter, who shared the same birthday as Jimmy Greaves, came later than most of us into the professional game. He had been labouring as a brick layer after Reading had turned down his written request for a trial. One of his uncles nagged Tommy Docherty into taking a look at him and, at seventeen, he was given a chance in the reserves. Twenty matches and thirty goals later he was promoted to the first team, scoring two goals in his debut against Workington in a League Cup tie in December 1964.

An Ossie goal was rarely ordinary. It usually followed a bewildering dribble and change of pace that would leave defenders floundering on their arses and goalkeepers diving the wrong way. I remember one goal against Burnley at Turf Moor in his first full season when he beat seven players in a sixty-yard run before rolling the ball into the net.

Ossie being Ossie, he could not resist taking the piss out of defenders and would deliberately nutmeg them and then go back and beat them again. It brought him a lot of sworn enemies, such as big Jack Charlton who could never get near him. He later admitted that Ossie's name was in his little black book of players he wanted to kick before he retired.

Peter was never malicious, but just full of fun and mischief. We never forgave Emlyn Hughes, who got his revenge for Ossie roasting him by breaking his leg with a vicious tackle in a League Cup tie at Blackpool that put Peter out of our 1967 FA Cup final against Tottenham.

But for that broken leg I am convinced Ossie would have won many more than his four England caps. Alf Ramsey admired him as a player, but was wary of him because of his playboy image. He included him in his 1970 World Cup squad, but only allowed him two appearances as a substitute.

Peter was a party animal, loved the ladies and liked to drink more than his fair share, along with good mates like Alan Hudson, Tommy Baldwin, Charlie Cooke and Ian Hutchinson. He was the most generous of people, and when you were on the point of

losing your temper with him he would disarm you with his big friendly grin and shrug of the shoulders.

It is a well-documented how he scored in every round of the 1970 FA Cup including the final – the last player to achieve the feat – and his diving header from Charlie Cooke's pass at Old Trafford is stuck in my memory as one of the greatest goals I ever saw. That goal showed that Peter had enormous bravery to go with his skill.

He was the difference between us and Real Madrid in the Cup Winners' Cup in Athens, and his attacking partnership with Ian Hutchinson was as lethal a combination as there was in the League.

Peter and I spent hours on the golf course together, and I rarely knew him as low as when the then chairman Ken Bates banned him (and me) from the Bridge for no real reason that we could understand. He had left Chelsea in controversial circumstances after he and Huddy had fallen out with the coach Dario Gradi and following a series of arguments with clean-living Dave Sexton over their lifestyles.

Alan went to Stoke and Ossie was all set to join him when Lawrie McMenemy moved in and stole him for Southampton for a then club record £275,000, while Chelsea fans were picketing the ground to try to keep their idol at the Bridge.

Ossie teamed-up with Mike Channon and ex-Chelsea player Jim McCalliog at Southampton, and they pulled off what was considered the impossible by beating Tommy Docherty's Manchester United in the 1976 FA Cup final.

Saints somehow managed to put the treasured FA Cup trophy in the keeping of the old King of the King's Road after the match. Ossie, of course, had plenty of partying experience at Chelsea to call on, and was leading the celebrations when suddenly entrusted with the job of making sure the FA Cup got back safely to Southampton. It was like putting a clown in charge of the circus.

So it was that at three o'clock on the morning after the final a seriously sozzled Ossie was showing off the FA Cup to astonished Saints supporters having a coffee at a mobile snackbar on the A3. Then, as you do, Ossie took the Cup home and slept with it! 'It was the best way of looking after it and keeping it safe,' Ossie later told me with the sort of logic that made sense only to him. What a character.

After a loan spell with Norwich, Ossie had a mad year in the United States playing for the Philadelphia Fury, with Alan Ball and Johnny Giles among his team-mates. "I decided to come home," he told me. "when our opponents for one match arrived in a covered wagon, wearing stetsons and shooting blanks from guns as they were chased on to the pitch by redskins."

Peter came back for one more season at the Bridge, an unhappy reunion when the club was in turmoil. He retired in 1979 and became a popular after-dinner speaker and also a meeter and greeter at Chelsea after Bates had left and his ban had been lifted.

Ossie's spirit will always live on at his beloved Chelsea. His ashes are buried under the pitch at the Shed End. The King of Stamford Bridge is at home.

Born: Derby, August 4 1948

Died: September 19 2002

Career span: 1968-1976

Clubs: Chelsea (1968-76)
119 League games, 44 goals
Total games for Chelsea:
144, 58 goals

Won 2 England Under-23 caps

Chelsea honours: FA Cup (1970)

HOW tragic that Ian Hutchinson and Peter Osgood – inseparable on and off the pitch – have both gone within a few years of each other. At their peak, they were devastating – Ossie all style and craft, Hutch a ferocious battering-ram of a player. They were so close they used to call each other 'bruv' and went into business together after their retirements from football.

I am breaking the rules putting Hutch in my Top 50 list because he did not play more than 150 games for Chelsea, but if anybody deserves to get an honours mention for what he did for the club it's Ian.

Virtually every time he pulled on a Chelsea shirt after his first couple of seasons he had to play through a pain barrier. He was always having pre-match injections and swallowing pain killing tablets so that he could get out on to the pitch and play. His career was cursed by injuries, including two broken legs, a broken arm, a broken toe and persistent knee trouble that led to a series of operations. Yet every time he went on to the pitch he played like a demon, crashing through tackles and diving in where others feared to tread. Defenders found him a nightmare to mark because he did not know the meaning of surrender.

He came to the club in odd circumstances. The son of a Derby foundry worker, Ian was missed by the usual schoolboy scouting network and was playing for Cambridge United when spotted by our then assistant manager Ron Suart, who had gone to the game to watch a goalkeeper. He recommended him to Dave Sexton, who agreed a fee of £2,500 and plus the same again after he had played twelve first-team matches.

I remember him unleashing his trademark long throw-in for the first time in a League match and the Ipswich defenders were so confused that one of them managed to turn it into his own net. It became a great attacking weapon for us and, of course, set up David Webb's winning goal in the 1970 FA Cup final replay.

In that 1969-70 season he and Ossie scored 53 goals between them, and were hugely responsible for our success. Peter was the more prolific scorer, but he was first to give credit to Hutch for opening the way to goal with his bullocking challenges that meant the harrassed defenders were taking their eye off Ossie as he moved into unmarked

space. Ian's throws averaged more than thirty yards and, at the peak of his powers, reached an officially measured thirty seven and a half yards.

It was in the season following our FA Cup victory that the injuries started to catch up with Ian, and he missed the European Cup Winners' Cup. In the 1972-73 season he managed only four appearances, and it was obvious he was in big trouble.

He battled bravely but, finally, had to throw in the towel just before the start of the 1976-77 season. Ian was just 27. In his 144 League and Cup appearances for Chelsea he managed to find the net 58 times.

Briefly, he played for Dartford and then became Chelsea's commercial director. Later he and Ossie ran a pub together in Windsor and Ian became a cordon bleu chef. But his health was failing and he was warned several times about his drinking damaging his liver. He was 54 when he died, and a distraught Ossie said: "I feel as if I have lost a brother."

QUOTE UNQUOTE: Ian Hutchinson

After the 1970 FA Cup final victory over Leeds:
"When Webbie headed in the winner following my throw-in I could not have been happier had I put the ball into the net myself. It was a move we had rehearsed dozens of times at the training ground, and for it to come off in the most important game of my life is just unbelievable."

Born: Highbury, May 7 1951

Career span: 1970-1987

Clubs: Chelsea (1970-84)
272 League games, 13 goals
Luton Town (1984 loan)
2 League games
Crystal Palace (1984-86)
49 League games, 7 goals
Brentford (1986-87)
19 League games, 3 goals

Total League games:
342, 23 goals

MICKY DROY was the Ambling Alp of Chelsea, a gentle, bearded giant who looked much fiercer than he actually was in the middle of our defence. I used to tell Micky that he was a big softie because – unlike, for example, Ian Hutchinson – he would never play through pain, and often missed games because of niggling rather than crippling injuries.

He gave Chelsea dedicated service during what were worrying times for the club, when they seemed to be losing their way on and off the pitch. Micky was a regular in the defence in what became the yo-yo years. The team was relegated in 1974-75, promoted back to the First Division in 1976-77, relegated again in 1978-79 and then promoted again in 1983-84.

The 'Big Feller' had been spotted playing for Slough Town (he could hardly be missed!), and joined our first-team squad just as we were going off the boil after the FA Cup and European Cup Winners' Cup successes.

When he came on for his debut as a substitute in 1970, Geoffrey Green – famous footall writer with *The Times* – wrote: 'Micky Droy came into the game as if plugged into the mains of Castle Frankenstein ..."

At 6ft 4in and weighing around sixteen stone, Micky was certainly a sight to behold, and had boots so big they could have been used as lifeboats. I remember him posing for pictures sparring with Joe Bugner when he was British and European heavyweight champion in the early Seventies. I took the pee out of Mick, telling him that he couldn't punch his way out of a paper bag. Mind you, I made sure I was well out of hitting distance when I told him. He was a lovely bloke off the pitch, and used to accept the 'mickey' taking with a big grin. Because of his size, he was naturally a power in the air in both penalty areas and scored quite a few important goals with his head – and stopped many more as he stood like a man mountain in the middle of our defence.

The fans identified with Micky's often clumsy but always whole-hearted effort in what were turbulent times at the Bridge and elected him Chelsea Player of the Year in 1978.

He was at the Bridge for fifteen years before a brief loan spell with Luton Town.

Art Turner
2010

Micky finally left Chelsea in 1984, first signing for Crystal Palace and later Brentford, before moving back to non-league football with Dulwich Hamlet and then Kingstonian, where he later became manager.

He had been an electrician before becoming a professional footballer, and wisely kept his hand in throughout his playing career. By the time he left Chelsea he had already set-up an electrical company in Westminster, which he gradually developed with his chip-off-the-old-block son Steve – another giant. Twenty-five years down the line he had built the business into a flourishing wholesale company that he was able to sell at a good enough price to enable him to retire to a life in the sun in Florida.

QUOTE UNQUOTE: Micky Droy

"The fifteen mostly happy years I spent at Chelsea helped no end when I set up my business. Customers were always keen to talk about the matches they'd seen, and it gave me the chance to get them in the right mood to do business. There were loads of ups and downs in my time at the Bridge, and it was certainly never ever boring or predictable. The game has changed beyond recognition, and the money the players earn today is mind-blowing. The fans were always good to me, and I have only fond memories."

Born: Chelsea, June 21 1951

Career span: 1968-1985

Clubs: Chelsea (1968-74)
145 League games, 10 goals
Stoke City (1974-76) Arsenal
(1976-78) Stoke City (1984-85)
Total League games:
325, 19 goals

England caps: 2

Chelsea honours: European
Cup Winners' Cup (1971)

TO quote Dave Sexton: "If Alan Hudson could have passed a pub like he passed a football, he would have been one of the all-time greats." I am not telling tales out of school when I reveal that as well as being a brilliant ball artist Alan was a Class A piss artist.

He fuelled himself with alcohol like others use water, and there were several times when we used to have to push him under a shower to sober him up before training sessions. Huddy, Ossie, Cookie, Hutch, Sponge and a few others used to bring the worst out of each other off the pitch – and the best on it. They lacked discipline when it came to saying "no" to the next drink. I can't claim to be a goody two-shoes and did my share, but I was never in their league and preferred to drink on my own manor rather than in the King's Road, which was like a celebrity fishbowl. Their liking for booze drove the very sober Dave Sexton to distraction. They once staggered back to the ground after a lunchtime drinking school in a local restaurant that went on until tea-time. The newspapers were tipped off and there was hell to pay.

It all eventually led to Hudson being sold off to Stoke and Ossie to Southampton (after he had shaken hands with Stoke manager Tony Waddington on a deal). I think it was an escape for Stoke, because Huddy and Ossie were a terrible influence on each other. Or maybe that should be a terrible 'under the' influence.

Alan was born to play for Chelsea, brought up a goal kick's distance from the ground. Yet it was Fulham he first wanted to play for, but they turned him down as a schoolboy before he signed for Chelsea juniors. He was all set to make his first-team debut at sixteen, but an injury put him on the sidelines – the first of a series of injuries that haunted his career.

It was February 1 1969 before he finally made his bow, and he wished he hadn't. We were taken apart 5-0 by Southampton. That season he showed a footballing maturity beyond his years, bossing the midfield with a master class in close control and precise passing. With flair players like Ossie and Cookie to feed, he was in his element and played a huge part in getting us to third place in the League and through to the FA Cup

final against Leeds. Injury robbed him of a deserved place in the final, but he got some consolation by steering us to the European Cup Winners' Cup the following season.

Soon after he and Ossie fell out with coach Dario Gradi and Dave Sexton, and he was bombed out to Stoke in 1974 for £240,000. His Chelsea career was over at the age of just twenty-two.

He found another good partying club at Stoke, but delivered on the pitch and the championship-challenging team of the Waddington/Hudson era is considered one of the finest sides in the long history of the Potteries club.

Hud upset Alf Ramsey when refusing to travel with the England Under-23 team and was banned from international football until Don Revie took over. He was the outstanding player on the pitch when England beat world champions West Germany at Wembley, and had a big say in the 5-0 destruction of Cyprus.

And that was it. Two caps, when he was the most gifted midfield player in the country. His run of injuries and a fall out with Don Revie meant his England career was all over. He and Ossie won just six caps between them. What a joke.

Stoke ran into financial trouble and were forced to sell Huddy to Arsenal in December 1976 for £200,000. He helped the Gunners reach the 1978 FA Cup final where they went down to a shock 1-0 defeat by Ipswich.

He then fell out with Arsenal manager Terry Neill, and moved across the Pond to play for Seattle Sounders and in the indoor league with Cleveland Force.

A combination of too much booze, injuries and illness robbed him of much of his pace and precision, and he made little impact in late-career moves to Hercules in Spain, a brief spell back at the Bridge and then a nostalgic return to Stoke, where he dug down into his memory to provide the passes that helped them avoid First Division relegation in the 1983-84 season.

His retirement years have been cursed with alcoholism, and a car accident in which he narrowly survived death after being run over and almost crippled. Somehow he has come through it all, including bankruptcy and is hugely popular at Stoke where they remember him as a ball artist rather than a piss artist. He has been successful with several books, and is still warmly remembered at the Bridge despite savage criticism of the club in the Ken Bates era.

There will only ever be one Alan Hudson. I just wonder what he would have achieved without the booze?

QUOTE UNQUOTE: Alan Hudson

"I'm not going to be negative and waste my time having regrets. I loved my playing career, particularly the Chelsea and Stoke days. I've been lucky to have the supporters at both Chelsea and Stoke like me, and that means so much. I like to think I could play a bit and would love to do it all again."

THERE's a generation growing up who would not believe the state Chelsea were in during the late 1970s when the club was having to sell stars such as Alan Hudson and Peter Osgood to stay afloat. They got in such a financial mess building a stand that fans threw spare cash into oil drums around the ground to help keep the club alive.

In these days when Chelsea are awash with Abramovich's money, it is difficult to realise that Eddie McCreadie was told he did not have a penny to spend when he took over as manager after the club had been relegated in 1975.

The club debt stood at £3.4 million, and Eddie had to make do with the pros he had in the squad including yours truly – plus the youngsters who were coming up through the youth scheme. Gary Locke was one of the most solid, and dependable of the players, a right-back who provided great service during difficult times. He always gave 100 per cent, and was a steadying influence as we battled our way back to the First Division in Eddie's first (and only) season as manager.

One memory of Gary that makes me shudder is that his shoulders used to pop out of their sockets if he took a throw-in. Even this far down the road my eyes water when I think of his pain, and we had to make sure he didn't take any throws. Gary was an athletic player with a sharp turn of speed, a disciplined marker and was always looking to turn defence into attack with thoughtfully placed passes.

Ten of the players in our squad that promotion season were homegrown. Gary had blue blood, and was unlucky to establish himself in the first-team squad at a time when the club was broke. He was there throughout all the yo-yo years before moving on to Crystal Palace in 1983 after serving the club as a professional from 1971.

Gary later had a spell in Sweden, and then moved to New Zealand where he captained Napier City Rovers and helped them win the national League championship.

Aged thirty-seven, he had a wind-down season with Waikato United, who finished second in the League title race and runners-up in the national cup final.

He stayed on in New Zealand and became a high-powered newspaper advertising executive. I wonder what he makes of the millions being poured into Stamford Bridge today, when he knew only peanut days?

Born: Willesden, July 12 1954
Career span: 1971-1986

Clubs: Chelsea (1971-83)
272 League games, 3 goals
Crystal Palace (1983-86) 84
League games, 1 goal
Total League games:
356, 4 goals

Later played for Halmstads BK in Sweden and Napier City Rovers in New Zealand

Represented England Youth

Born: Hillingdon, September 14 1956
Career span: 1973-1997

Clubs: Chelsea (1973-79) 179 League games, 30 goals Manchester United (1979-84) AC Milan (1984-87) Paris Saint-Germain (1987) Rangers (1987-89) QPR (1989-94) Crystal Palace (1994) QPR (1994-1996) Wycombe Wanderers (1996) Hibernian (1996-97) Millwall (1997) Leyton Orient (1997) **Total League games:** 695, 49 goals

England caps: 84, 3 goals

Manager: QPR, Fulham, Chelsea. Chelsea assistant first-team coach (2009-)

I TOOK it as gracefully as possible when Eddie McCreadie gave my captain's armband to eighteen-year-old Ray 'Butch' Wilkins in 1975. I'd been proud to captain the club more times than any other Chelsea skipper, but I was approaching the veteran stage and Ray was the bright new future of the club we both loved.

I bet Terry Venables thought to himself when Butch was given the captaincy: "Now he knows how I felt when Tommy Doc took it away from me and handed it to a promising youngster."

At twenty-two, I had been Chelsea's youngest captain. Now Ray had knocked a hole in that record.

In his first season, he led the Blues back to the First Division and he thrived on his new responsibility. He played with a maturity beyond his years, and showed a great tactical brain and passing ability that made him stand out as a schemer who knew just what weight to put on the ball.

He deserved to have better players around him during what was a bleak period for the club, and I am convinced he would have stayed with Chelsea if there had been any hope on the horizon of some medals.

Ray must have thought I liked him a lot because during our training sessions I always made sure I stuck close to him, so that when it came to the sprints he made me look quick. The one thing Ray could never do was get up into a gallop, and his reluctance to push forward earned him two nicknames: Sideways Ray and The Crab.

The son of former professional George Wilkins, he and his two brothers Graham and Stephen all joined the Chelsea groundstaff from school. Ray was the finished article from the moment he stepped into senior football, and for four years he almost carried the first team with his stunning passing and ability to read situations faster than the players around him.

Hard to imagine when you look at him now, but in those early days he had an impressive shock of hair and was a handsome young man who was a regular pin-up in the teeny-bopper girlie magazines of the era. He was a good, clean-living boy and the

Art Turner
2010

drinking culture at the club had at last been squashed. Rather than a tequila, Ray was more likely to be seen drinking a Tango!

Dave Sexton had been manager when Ray first appeared at the club as a schoolboy and kept a close watch on him. At the first opportunity, he snapped him up for Manchester United with an £800,000 deal that was vital lifeblood for a Chelsea club then on its uppers.

He had his golden moments away from the Bridge, first at Old Trafford, then with AC Milan, Paris-Saint Germain and later back in the UK with Glasgow Rangers and QPR. Ray also made fleeting appearances for Crystal Palace, Wycombe, Hibs, Millwall and Leyton Orient.

The Eighties was his decade and he became a fixture in the England midfield, winning 84 caps. One of his career highlights came during Euro 1980 in Italy when he scored a cracking goal against Belgium in a group match. He lobbed the ball over the Belgian defence, ran forward to collect the ball himself and then lobbed it again, this time over the goalkeeper's head and into the net. It made all of us in the game wonder why he did not score many more goals. If his legs had been as quick as his brain he would have been one of the greatest midfield players ever.

An accomplished broadcaster, he's been a regular pundit on television but his main employment has been through management at QPR and Fulham, where he worked with Kevin Keegan. Fulham chairman Al Fayed sacked him following a poor run of results, and Keegan was given his job. It led to, let's say, a cooling of the friendship between the two former England team-mates.

In recent seasons, Ray has had two brief spells as caretaker boss at the Bridge and coach and all-knowing assistant to the parade of foreign managers who have filled the Chelsea hot seat.

As I watch him shouting instructions from the touchline I smile to myself as I think how the bushy-haired Butch has become completely bald and looking like a villain in a James Bond film.

All in all the boy's done good.

QUOTE UNQUOTE: Ray Wilkins

"I often wonder how we would have got on in my playing days at Chelsea if we'd had the stability and wealth that Mr Abramovich has brought to the club. The club was in turmoil when I was pitched into taking the captain's job when I was just eighteen. I grew up overnight, and thrived on the responsibility. It was a wrench for me to leave when Dave Sexton took me to Man United, but it was the right thing for my career at the time. Back then, I would never have believed that Chelsea could develop into one of the most successful and powerful clubs in the world."

CLIVE was one of the great Chelsea characters, who brought smiles to faces during what were often bad times at the Bridge. He was out of the old school of wingers, with pace and power that used to have full-backs working overtime to try to keep up with him.

Most of his peak Chelsea times were spent in the Second Division, when the club was battling with debts off the pitch and indifferent performances on it. His enthusiasm used to light up matches and lift the fans, whose loyalty in those hungry years was remarkable.

Older fans still recall his outstanding performances against the then European champions Liverpool in FA Cup ties in 1979 and 1982. He scored twice in the first match to set up a 4-2 victory, and in the second game teed-up a late victory-clinching goal for Colin Lee.

> **Born: Oxford, May 26 1957**
> **Career span: 1976-1999**
>
> **Clubs: Chelsea (1976-1984) 198 League games, 60 goals Sunderland (1984-86) QPR (1986-87) Fulham (1987-90) Brighton & Hove Albion (1990-93)**
> **Played 203 non-League games for Woking before finishing his career at Cheltenham Town**
> **Total League games: 484, 108 goals**
>
> **Represented England Schools**

He is perhaps best remembered for the goal that saved Chelsea from sliding down into the Third Division in 1982-83. He kept the Blues up with a goal in the closing minutes of the penultimate match of the season against fellow strugglers Bolton Wanderers. Chelsea historians will tell you that it was possibly one of the most vital goals ever scored for the club. It kept them from a relegation that could have sent them into financial meltdown.

Clive, who had a spell on loan with Fort Lauderdale Strikers in 1979, left the club under a cloud in 1983-84 when he signed for Sunderland following a contract dispute. The following season he came back to haunt his old club. He was the inspiration behind Sunderland's 5-2 aggregate victory over Chelsea in the League Cup semi-final. Feelings were stoked so high that there was a near riot and a fan invaded the pitch and chased the former Bridge hero after he had dismantled the Blues defence.

It did not end happily for Clive. He missed from the penalty spot in the final at Wembley and Norwich City won 1-0.

Clive later played for QPR, Fulham and Brighton, and became a cult hero when playing into his 40s with Woking and Cheltenham. He has become a radio broadcaster, and set up a *Sporting Experience* company with ex-Chelsea team-mate Jason Cundy.

Born: Glenrothes, February 20 1960
Career span: 1978-1994

Clubs: Barnsley (1978-80) Darlington (1980-82) Chelsea (1982-87) 162 League games, 47 goals Coventry (1987-91) Liverpool (1991) Blackburn (1991-92) Southampton (1992-93) Birmingham City (loan 1992) WBA (loan 1992) West Ham (loan 1993) Leicester (1993-94) Total League games: 519, 148 goals

Scotland caps: 10

I HAD ended my 21-year association with Chelsea by the time David Speedie arrived from Darlington in 1982. He made a mega impact at the Bridge, and forged a partnership with Kerry Dixon that was rated the most dynamic attacking duo since the days of Osgood and Hutchinson. In his 204 appearances for the Blues he scored 64 goals, including a hat-trick against Manchester City at Wembley in the 1986 Full Members Cup final. It was the first hat-trick at Wembley since the historic treble by Geoff Hurst twenty years earlier in the 1966 World Cup final.

Speedie was not particularly pretty on the eye, but was strong on the ball and had good stamina and was always eager to get into the box. He was a nasty little sod who was often in trouble with referees, but he gave Chelsea the competitive edge that had been lacking in previous seasons. He shared with Greavsie and Ossie February 20 as his birthday.

Everything was going well for him in the 1980s when he won the first of ten caps for Scotland in a 1-0 victory over England. In 1983-84, Chelsea were never out of the top three in their chase for promotion back to the First Division. Speedie, incredibly good in the air for such a small feller, linked perfectly with Dixon and fellow-Scot Pat Nevin. Chelsea had the best travelling suppport in the Second Division – and better than most of the clubs in the First – and they rewarded the fans with a 5-0 thrashing of Leeds to make certain of going up, and then in the final game of the season they beat Grimsby to clinch the Second Division title. Throughout that promotion season they lost only four League matches and Speedie was without doubt one of their most consistent players.

His world turned sour when he fell out big time with rookie manager John Hollins. It got out of hand to the point where Speedie demanded a transfer and made blistering criticisms of John, who had no other option than to drop him into the reserves, when he needed him on full power in the first-team.

He was eventually sold to Coventry for £750,000 in the summer of 1987, much

to the despair of many Chelsea fans who loved his goal plundering alongside Kerry Dixon. Speedie became a nomadic player after leaving the Bridge, appearing in the shirt of Coventry, Liverpool, Blackburn, Southampton, Birmingham City, West Brom, West Ham and Leicester City. Early in his career he had played for Barnsley and Darlington, so that was eleven League clubs in all.

After his retirement, he ran a recruitment company and represented players as an agent. I wonder what advice he would have given himself during his dispute with John Hollins? He needed somebody to talk sense to him, so that he could have realised that his best decision would have been to stay at Chelsea where he was worshipped by the supporters.

QUOTE UNQUOTE: David Speedie

"My happiest days at Chelsea were when John Neal was manager. He brought a great atmosphere to the dressing-room and training ground and used to smile so much we called him Jolly John. I could not say the same about his successor John Hollins. I always believed in speaking my mind, so was sometimes not the most popular of people. But that's the way I am. I never could stand the whispering behind backs. Our promotion-winning team had the balance just right and we went into every game with a feeling of confidence and belief in each other."

NIGEL was the heart of that outstanding Chelsea team of the mid-Eighties that pumped the pride and passion back into the club – just as it seemed the Blues could go out of business because of the pressure of off-field debts.

He arrived from Bournemouth as a £35,000 plank in John Neal's rebuilding of the side along with the likes of Kerry Dixon, Pat Nevin and David Speedie. Nigel scored on his debut for Chelsea in a 5-0 opening day win over Derby County, one of only 12 goals in 208 League games for the club. It was a flying start to the season that ended with Chelsea promoted as champions.

Full of industry and enthusiasm, Nigel was the piston in the midfield engine room. He made the team tick with his unselfish running, willingly fetching and carrying for the better ball players around him and working brilliantly in tandem with the always reliable John Bumstead.

Born: Romsey, Hampshire December 2 1960
Career span: 1980-1998
Clubs:
Bournemouth (1980-1983)
Chelsea (1983-87/1992-96)
208 League games, 12 goals
Liverpool (1987-89)
QPR (1989) Rangers (1989-92) Sheffield United (1996-98)
Total League games:
521, 24 goals

Manager: Sheffield United (player-manager 1997-98)
Barnsley (2001) Millwall (2006)

He had two spells at the Bridge, never giving anything less than 100 per cent – apart from during the period when he along with David Speedie and Joe McLaughlin had a war of words with manager John Hollins. Several players mouthed off to the tabloid press, but Spackman kept his feelings to himself. It all led to a sour atmosphere in the camp and he was shifted out to Liverpool in a £400,000 deal in 1987. Just as at the Bridge, Nigel was content to be a team player and he quickly became identified as an unsung hero by the Kop.

After Anfield, Nigel played for Queens Park Rangers and Glasgow Rangers before a return to the Bridge that was handicapped by a recurring back problem. In 1996 he moved to Sheffield United where he became player-manager. He had brief experiences as manager at Barnsley and Millwall before starting on a new career as a TV football pundit, including regular appearances on a Singapore channel carrying Premier League football. Hospitality rooms at Stamford Bridge were named Speedie and Spackman, and there was huge controversy in 2009 when Nigel confessed that Liverpool was the club closest to his heart. A lot of Chelsea fans got the blues with him over that admission.

Born: Luton, July 24 1961

Career span: 1980-1997

Clubs: Reading (1980-83)
Chelsea (1983-92)
335 League games, 147 goals
Southampton (1992-93) Luton
Town (1993-95) Millwall
(1995-96) Watford (1996)
Doncaster Rovers (player-
manager 1996-97)
Total League games:
593, 231 goals

England caps: 8, 4 goals

THE fact that Kerry Dixon scored more goals for Chelsea than even Greavsie says all that needs to be said as to why he is and will always be a legend at the Bridge. Only Bobby Tambling has scored more than his 193 League and Cup goals for the club.

What a cock-up Spurs made when they let him go after he had served his apprenticeship at White Hart Lane. He played non-League football with Chesham United and Dunstable before starting his League career with Reading.

John Neal knew he had discovered gold when he watched Dixon lead the Reading line, but chairman Ken Bates had to be persuaded that it was worth paying out a £150,000 transfer fee plus an extra £25,000 if Kerry ever got capped by England. Neal finally got his man and brought him into his new-look squad at the Bridge along with Pat Nevin, Nigel Spackman, Joe McLaughlin and Eddie Niedzwiecki.

Dixon made an instant impact, banging in two goals on his debut against Derby County and he added 32 more in one of the club's most exciting seasons as they powered to promotion as Second Division champions.

It is part of Chelsea folklore how Chelsea clinched promotion with a 5-0 win against Leeds United, a game in which Dixon helped himself to a hat-trick. He had struck up a potent partnership with fiery Scot David Speedie, ironing out differences after disliking each other on sight. They put the team cause above their personal feud and were a double handful for the tightest defences. The pair linked brilliantly with Scottish winger Pat Nevin, and over the next three years the Terrible Trio scored almost 200 goals between them.

The strong and athletic Dixon showed the following season that he could also score on the First Division stage, finishing joint top 24-goalscorer with Gary Lineker as Chelsea came a creditable sixth in the final table. In the same season, he collected a further eight goals in the League Cup as Chelsea reached the semi-finals, where they surprisingly lost to Sunderland. He was on fire in those first two seasons and scored a total of 70 goals in just 101 games. It was electrifying stuff.

Chelsea challenged for the title in the 1985-86 season but Dixon was handicapped halfway through by torn stomach muscles and they finished sixth again.

This was as good as it got for the 1980s Chelsea team, and they lost their way following a series of bad-tempered clashes between key players and John Hollins and his management team.

The side was broken up and Dixon was dropped. He was close to signing for Arsenal until Ken Bates made a last-minute intervention and insisted he stay at Chelsea. By then Dixon had won eight England caps in a stuttering international career that finished after a brief appearance in the 1986 World Cup finals.

He rediscovered his goal touch after Chelsea were relegated in 1988, and netted 25 League goals as the Blues blasted their way straight back to the top table. A year later he scored a further 26 goals, including a final day hat-trick against Millwall, lifting Chelsea to fifth in the table, their highest First Division position since 1970.

Kerry moved to Southampton in 1992 in a £575,000 deal and briefly linked-up again with Speedie, but they failed to produce their old magic. He played for his hometown club Luton, then Millwall and Watford before a season as player-manager of Doncaster Rovers, without ever getting near the form that once made him Chelsea's Mr Dynamite. He coached non-League sides Boreham Wood, Letchworth and Hitchin Town, and set up a coaching school in Dunstable. I sometimes see him these days at the Bridge when we are both on matchday hospitality duty, and you can almost feel the respect the fans have for him. He is popular on Chelsea TV, and can look any of the Chelsea greats in the eye because at his peak he was as good as it gets.

QUOTE UNQUOTE: Kerry Dixon

"We were really flying in those first couple of seasons. Speedo and I settled our personal differences and got on with finding the net as often as possible. The stomach injury I got against Liverpool was much more serious than I first thought, and it took me a long time to get my old pace back, and then the team started breaking up and we couldn't get it together again."

Born: Saltcoats, Scotland August 29 1963

Career span: 1982-1998

Clubs: St Mirren (1982-1987) Chelsea (1987-98) 330 League games, 7 goals

Chelsea honours: FA Cup (1997) League Cup (1998) European Cup Winners' Cup (1998)

Scotland caps: 6

Coaching roles: Newcastle United (caretaker manager 1999), Chelsea (assistant manager 2004-08) West Ham United (assistant manager 2008-10)

STEVE was out of my school of defenders, and did not believe in taking any prisoners with his uncompromising challenges. He was the heartbeat of Chelsea while making more than 400 League and Cup appearances, and was equally effective at right-back or in the centre of the defence.

For all his power and brute force, Steve was always a thinking footballer and he put his tactical knowledge to good use when he became a top-quality coach, including long service as a vital member of the Stamford Bridge backroom team.

'Clarkey' was signed for £400,000 from St Mirren by John Hollins and made his debut as a substitute in a 2-2 draw at Norwich. He arrived at a testing time at Chelsea, when several of the key players were at loggerheads with the management team. But Steve settled down and just got on with his job as he proved he was an outstanding professional in attitude and application.

There was a definite improvement in team performances as the players responded to Steve's total commitment, and his 100 per cent effort was rewarded when he was selected along with his team-mate and countryman Pat Nevin for a Football League XI against a World XI featuring Diego Maradona and Michel Platini at Wembley in August 1987. The match was part of the Football League's Centenary celebrations, and the experience was invaluable for when Steve stepped on to the international stage for six caps with Scotland.

Highlights of his eleven-year Chelsea career were winning the club's Player of the Year award in 1994, and being part of the Chelsea sides which captured the FA Cup, League Cup and European Cup Winners' Cup in the late 1990s. The Cup Winners' Cup final, against VfB Stuttgart in Stockholm, was Clarkey's final appearance for the club. He went out at the top, but already with a future mapped out as a coach.

In 2005 he won a place in Chelsea's Centenary XI, voted in as right-back. To be honest, I would have given that shirt to Ken Shellito but I suppose the fact that his

career was cut short by injury meant he had not had time to cement himself into Chelsea memories.

After retiring in 1998 he had a spell as coach and assistant to Rudd Gullit at Newcastle and then caretaker manager before returning to the Bridge to become a coach respected and liked by all the players. Jose Mourinho allowed him a big say in tactics and he continued to be influential as managers came and went. Chelsea tried to prevent him following Gianfranco Zola to West Ham. They finally relented and got a fat fee, but he had two less than successful seasons as Zola's right-hand man at Upton Park before following Gianfranco out of the Hammers door in 2010. A man with his coaching skills is certain to be in demand.

QUOTE UNQUOTE: Steve Clarke

"My days as a player at Chelsea were, to say the least, eventful. I was always interested in the coaching side of things, and it was natural for me to move into that area when I retired. Tactics have held a fascination for me from way back, and my ambition is to one day put my ideas into operation as a club manager. It was a great honour to get into the Chelsea Centenary team. That was a side I would loved to have coached!"

Born: Glasgow,
September 6 1963

Career span: 1981-2000

Clubs: Clyde (1981-1983)
Chelsea (1983-88)
193 League games, 36 goals
Everton (1988-92)
Tranmere Rovers (1992-97)
Kilmarnock (1997-98)
Motherwell (1998-2000)
Total League games:
660, 107 goals

Scotland caps: 28, 5 goals

Motherwell chief executive
(1999-2002)

PAT was a polished perfectionist of a winger, the type of player I would have been looking to put into Row Z before he could take control of the match. He was not quite as clever with the ball at his feet as Eddie Gray, but he had a good brain on him and was a force down the touchlines and in midfeld.

His 20-year playing career kicked off at Clyde after Celtic had let him go because they said he was too small to make the grade. Wrong! In his first season, he helped Clyde win promotion as Scottish Second Division champions, scoring twelve goals and winning the vote as young player of the year.

He arrived at the Bridge in the summer of 1983 for £95,000 as John Neal created a new Chelsea. His untried team-mates included Kerry Dixon, Nigel Spackman, David Speedie and Eddie Niedzwiecki. Nevin was a vital piece in the Neal jigsaw because he had the ball skill and pace to to feed Dixon and fellow-Scot Speedie with vital passes.

Nevin quickly became a key player and a favourite with the fans, who identified with his quality and his enthusiasm. As well as creating dozens of chances for his team-mates in the promotion season of 1983-84, he also scored 14 goals. He produced a string of dazzling performances, leaving defenders chasing his shadow and was not only rewarded with a Second Division championship medal but also the Chelsea Player of the Year award.

He continued his impressive raids down the wing as Chelsea finished a satisfactory sixth in the First Division the following year and reached the Milk Cup semi-finals. He was particularly outstanding against Sheffield Wednesday in the quarter-finals as Chelsea came back from 3-0 down to draw 4-4, and it was Pat who set up the winner for Speedie in the replay.

The Blues made a spirited challenge for the championship the next season, with Nevin scoring a late equaliser against Liverpool at Anfield and a vital headed goal against West Ham United to clinch a 2-1 win. The team lost its way in the 1987-

88 season because of unrest in the dressing-room and at the training ground, but Nevin continued to play his heart out and was again voted Player of the Year as Chelsea slipped back into the Second Division.

Chelsea urgently needed money and they reluctantly sold Nevin to Everton for £925,000. He scored 20 goals in 138 appearances for the Merseysiders, but was never the same force as at Chelsea. He later played with distinction for Tranmere before winding down his career back home in Scotland with Kilmarnock and then Motherwell. He had two years as Motherwell's chief executive before leaving just ahead of the decision to call in the administrators.

An intelligent man with an arts degree from Glasgow Caledonian University, he turned his attention to the media, and he continues to work extensively in television, as a newspaper columnist and author. He co-authored a book called *In Ma Head, Son* – a study of the psychology of football.

Wonder what he would have made of me wanting to put him over the touchline? It was a different game in my day, but Pat would no doubt have had me down as a head case. I just did what I thought was necessary for the team.

QUOTE UNQUOTE: Pat Nevin

"Football is a strange game. You get together with 20 other people in a squad and, even though you have nothing in common off the pitch, you have to get to know each other like family on the field of play. For a couple of years at Chelsea, we all just clicked. We instinctively knew where each of us would be and what to do. It was a special time. If we'd had a couple more seasons together as a unit we could have achieved so much more."

**Born: Paisley, Scotland
December 6 1965**

Career span: 1981-2001

**Clubs: East Fife (1981-1984)
Hibernian (1984-86)
Chelsea (1986-91)
123 League games, 51 goals
Tottenham Hotspur (1991-93)
Rangers (1993-2000) Hearts
(2000-01)
Total League games:
450, 149 goals**

Scotland caps: 43, 7 goals

UNDER-the-cosh John Hollins brought in Gordon 'Juke Box' Durie to shake up the dynamic duo Kerry Dixon and David Speedie in April 1986. They had seen off the challenge of under-achieving Welshman Gordon Davies a year earlier, but Durie looked the business when he arrived from Hibernian for £380,000.

He was an unsmiling no-nonsense, get-on-with-it pro, who the press described as "burly and surly." Gordon had a good physique, could really motor, packed a powerful shot and was strong in the air. At first he was played in a three-pronged attack with Dixon and Speedie, but they got in each other's way.

It was only after the departure of Speedie that Gordon came into his own, playing a barnstorming role alongside Dixon. His dead-ball shots were feared by goalkeepers, and his enthusiasm and desire to be a winner lifted the players around him. Chelsea went right off the boil when he was sidelined with a knee injury, and they were relegated in what were then high-pressure play-offs.

Chelsea failed to win one of their opening six games of their season back in the Second Division, but a thumping shot from Durie at Leeds triggered their first victory and there was then no stopping them.

He and Dixon suddenly clicked together. It was not as smooth as the Dixon-Speedie combination, but was just as lethal. Jukebox scored twice in a 5-0 victory over Plymouth, collected another two goals in a 4-1 victory at Birmingham and then – in a 7-0 win at Walsall – he became the first Chelsea player since the days of Jimmy Greaves and Bobby Tambling to score five goals in a game.

He was handicapped by injury for much of the season but still netted 17 goals as Chelsea galloped away with the Second Division title.

The return to the top table proved a season of misery for Gordon, who spent more time on the treatment table than on the pitch. But when fit he was awesome, scoring 12 times in 24 League matches including both goals in a 2-0 victory over QPR, the winning goal at home to Tottenham, another two in an astonishing 6-4 win at Derby and a spectacular goal in a 3-2 defeat of Manchester United at the Bridge.

Art Turner
2010

Optimism was high when he scored again in a 4-2 home end-of-season victory over Liverpool. But then came the bombshell news that because his wife was homesick for Scotland he was going to have to leave the club. He got his wish to be nearer Scotland by moving north for £2.2 million … to Tottenham in North London!

Capped 43 times by Scotland, Durie failed to make an impact at White Hart Lane as a partner for Gary Lineker and, after two seasons, moved back home to Scotland, where he became a key man in helping Rangers in their nine League titles in-a-row run. He scored a hat-trick in the 1996 Scottish Cup final in a 5-1 victory over Hearts, the club with which he had a winding-down season in 2000-01.

These days Gordon does occasional football punditry work and coaches at the magnificent Murray Park training complex where his son, Scott, is in the Rangers youth squad as a centre-back.

QUOTE UNQUOTE: Gordon Durie

"I had terrible injury problems that spoiled my stay at Chelsea, but I've fond memories of some great games and great results. The story about my wife wanting us to be nearer Scotland was perfectly true at the time, but then Spurs came in with an offer neither Chelsea nor I could refuse. It didn't work out like I expected, and I went home for the best years of my playing career with Rangers during what was a golden era for the club."

Born: Oliena, July 5 1966
Career span: 1984-2005

Clubs: Nuorese (1984-86)
Torres (1986-89) Napoli
(1989-93) Parma (1993-96)
Chelsea (1996-2003)
229 League games, 59 goals
Cagliari (2003-05)
League games: 629, 193 goals

Chelsea honours: FA Cup
(1997, 2000) European Cup
Winners' Cup (1998) League
Cup (1998)

**1997 FWA Footballer of the
Year**

Italy caps: 35, 10 goals

Manager: West Ham United
(2008-10)

GIANFRANCO put smiles on Chelsea faces at one of their saddest times. He made his debut against Tottenham just three days after popular director Matthew Harding had died in a helicopter crash, and he got an instant rapport with the Stamford Bridge fans with his stunning skill and almost relaxed attitude. By the time he had finished his Chelsea career he was a Blues legend and was voted the club's greatest ever player.

Zola signed from Parma for £4.5 million in November 1996 as Ruud Gullit marked his management with sweeping and revolutionary changes that meant the Bridge would never be quite the same again. The club was suddenly unrecognizable from the one with which I had grown up and played for more than twenty years, and even this old git has to admit they were suddenly exciting times.

Wearing the No. 25 shirt, he continually took the eye and the headlines with some astonishing performances in his first season. One goal against Manchester United in February 1997 – when he ran rings round the United defence – had Alex Ferguson shaking his head in wonder and saying: "He's a clever little so-and-so …"

Gianfranco was the motivator of the team that won the FA Cup for the first time since our 1970 victory over Leeds. His input included four goals on the way to the final, and two of them were extra-special. He shocked Liverpool with a bending shot from 25 yards as Chelsea came from 0-2 down to win 4-2. Then, in the semi-final against Wimbledon, he spun on a sixpence to collect his own back-heel and steer the ball into the net. No wonder at the end of his three-quarters of a season he was voted the FWA Footballer of the Year – the first Chelsea player to win the coveted award.

He was prominent again in 1997-98 when he helped Chelsea win three more trophies – the League Cup, the European Cup Winners' Cup and the Super Cup. Carrying an injury in the Cup Winners' Cup final against Stuttgart in Stockholm, he came on as a second-half substitute and scored the winning goal just 21 seconds after stepping on to

QUOTE UNQUOTE: Gianfranco Zola

"I was very nervous at first about joining Chelsea. It was a very big step for me after spending all my career playing in Italy. But I was made to feel at home from the very first minute, and I will have a special place in my heart for the club and the supporters until the day I die."

the pitch. With only his second touch of the game, he rifled a through ball from Dennis Wise into the roof of the net to clinch Chelsea's third major trophy in a year and the second European trophy in the club's history. Ah, memories of Athens.

In the same season, Zola collected the first hat-trick of his career in a 4-0 victory over Derby County at Stamford Bridge in November 1997. Standing only 5ft 6in tall, he was proving himself a giant of the game - just as he had in Italy, where he won 35 international caps and learned many of his tricks playing alongside Diego Maradona at Napoli.

Ruud Gullit had parted company with the club by the time Chelsea made their first challenge for the Champions League in 1999-2000. Zola was a key player throughout the campaign but his appearances in the League were limited because of new manager Gianluca Vialli's squad-rotation system.

The little master scored three goals in Chelsea's run to the quarter-finals, including a curling free-kick against Barcelona, and he again won the FA Cup with the club when it was his free-kick in the final against Aston Villa that set up Roberto Di Matteo's winner.

He had a brief, electric partnership with Jimmy Floyd Hasselbaink before the arrival of Claudio Ranieri as manager. Eidur Gudjohnsen was preferred most of the time alongside Jimmy, but one incredible back-heeled goal while in mid-air against Norwich in the FA Cup had Ranieri saying: "He is a wizard … that was fantasy, absolute magic."

Just when people were writing Gianfranco off as over the top, he scored sixteen goals in his final season of 2002-03 and was again voted the club's Player of the Year after helping Chelsea qualify for the Champions League. His final goal said it all about his imagination, skill and cheek when he lobbed Everton goalkeeper Richard Wright from outside the penalty area.

In 2003, Zola was voted the best ever Chelsea player by the Bridge fans and in November 2004, he was awarded an OBE – Honorary Member of the Order of the British Empire in a special ceremony in Rome.

He returned to Italy to play for Cagliari, just ahead of the Chelsea takeover by Russian billionaire Roman Abramovich who was so keen to get Gianfranco back to the Bridge that it was strongly rumoured he offered to buy the entire Cagliari club!

Zola steered Cagliari back to Serie A before retiring to concentrate on coaching as assistant manager of the Italian Under-21 team. He was then tempted back to England as manager of West Ham, which brought his first unhappy spell in football and a sacking after two years of struggle. But he is too much of a football genius to be kept down for long.

Glad I never had to mark – as Fergie said – "the little so-and-so …"

DESPITE his small physique, Dennis was famed and feared for his combative style of play with which I could easily identify. His tackling and fierce competitive spirit was a constant source of inspiration to his team-mates and an aggravation to opponents.

He came to the Bridge from the notorious Wimbledon 'Crazy Gang' club, where dressing-room pranks and an all-for-one-and-one-for-all spirit was the foundation for their unexpected success in the late 1980s. It was a Wise cross that opened the way for the shock headed winning goal from Lawrie Sanchez against Liverpool that won the FA Cup for the Dons in 1988.

It cost Chelsea a then club record £1.6 million to capture him, and his drive and determination won him instant favour with the fans. From the moment he took over the captaincy in 1993 he bossed matches from midfield as he brought the best out of the more gifted foreign players surrounding him.

Born: Kensington December 16 1966
Career span: 1985-2006

Clubs: Wimbledon (1985-90) Chelsea (1990-2001)
332 League games, 53 goals Leicester (2001-02) Millwall (2002-05), Southampton (2005-06), Coventry (2006) Total League games: 593, 95 goals

Chelsea honours: FA Cup (1997, 2000) European Cup Winners' Cup (1998) League Cup (1998)

England caps: 21, 1 goal

Manager: Millwall, Southampton, Swindon, Leeds

Originally signed from Wimbledon as a wide man, be became more influential after a switch to central midfield. He thrived on the extra responsibility and within a year of taking the captain's armband he had led Chelsea to an FA Cup final victory, the first of six trophies he lifted in just four seasons. He was Chelsea's most successful captain until John Terry came along, helped by shovelfuls of Abramovich's money.

He was a strong supporter on and off the pitch to Ruud Gullit as player/manager and, on the arrival of foreign imports Roberto Di Matteo, Gianluca Vialli, Frank Leboeuf and Gianfranco Zola, Wise went out of his way to help each of them bed in at the Bridge.

Dennis made 445 Chelsea appearances and scored 76 goals. He would have comfortably topped the 500 game mark if he had not collected a string of yellow and red cards.

He was a controversial figure on and off the pitch, and sometimes made headlines away from the back pages with behaviour that was claimed to bring the club into disrepute.

86 Chopper's Chelsea

In 1995 he was convicted of assaulting a London taxi-driver and given a three-month prison sentence, which was later overturned on appeal. Four years later he was accused of 'biting' Marcelino Elena of RCD Mallorca in a Cup Winners' Cup tie and in the 1998–99 season he missed a total of 15 games through suspension. Man United manager Alex Ferguson famously said of him: "That Wise could start a fight in an empty house."

Despite his disciplinary record, he was still in demand by England and won 21 caps over a period of ten years. He scored once, on his debut against Turkey on May 1 1991 when he was with Wimbledon. Dennis played in all three group games for England at Euro 2000, against Portugal (lost 2–3), Germany (won 1–0) and Romania (lost 2–3). His value to the team was as a holding player, and he would have been just what the doctor ordered for Fabio Capello's England at the 2010 World Cup finals. He could win the ball and then deliver it to a team-mate all in one swift movement that would keep the flow and rhythm of a move going.

But eventually at Chelsea he got overtaken by younger imports and, in the summer of 2001, new manager Claudio Ranieri decided to let him go after making it clear he was looking to lower the average age of the squad.

He joined Leicester City for £1.6 million, a move that became clouded in yet more controversy when he was sacked after breaking a team-mate's jaw in a fight.

He later played for Millwall, Southampton and Coventry City, gradually switching to the managerial side of the game after player-manager experience with Millwall and Southampton, where he had started his career as an apprentice more than twenty years earlier. He was in charge at Swindon and then Leeds before switching to an executive director role at Newcastle United.

Dennis got himself involved in political unrest at St James' Park and finally left Newcastle in April 2009 after many months of boardroom and dressing-room friction. He bided his time working with non-League Chalfont St Peter while waiting for the chance to return to the game at ownership level. Charlton Athletic was one club he had his eye on as leader of a syndicate with Middle East financial backing. That deal fell through, but there is a lot more yet to come from Dennis Wise.

QUOTE UNQUOTE: Dennis Wise

"They were really exciting days at Chelsea when we won six trophies in four years. I felt privileged to be captaining a team packed with players of tremendous skill. Some of them couldn't understand a word I was saying but we all spoke the same football language. That Chelsea side of the mid-90s was as good as ever been seen in England, and it was beyond my dreams that I was the captain picking up the cups. Tremendous times!"

Born: Bucharest, Romania December 22 1967

Career span: 1985-2003

Clubs: Steaua Bucharest, Foggia, Genoa, Sheffield Wednesday, Chelsea (1995-2000) 151 League games, 17 goals Bradford City, Southampton, Progresul Bucharest Total League games: 436, 59 goals

Chelsea honours: FA Cup (1997) European Cup Winners' Cup (1998) League Cup (1998)

Romania caps: 95, 12 goals

DAN PETRESCU will always be remembered at the Bridge for being the first overseas player to reach 100 appearances for Chelsea, and also for the manner of his leaving after a blazing row with manager Gianluca Vialli.

He had arrived in December 1995 from Sheffield Wednesday, signed by Glenn Hoddle as a wing-back encouraged to play from deep with a positive attitude.

Petrescu, capped 95 times by Romania, was a class act. He had played in the 1989 European Cup final for Steaua Bucharest and had been a key player in the Romania side that reached the World Cup quarter-finals in 1994, and he gathered vital experience with two Italian clubs, Foggia and Genoa. He was a talented player in the Hoddle mould, and Glenn had been on his trail for months.

Dan settled comfortably into the Hoddle system, and he became even more of an influence on the team when Glenn departed to be replaced by player-manager Ruud Gullit.

He switched to his favourite position of right-sided midfielder in a 4-4-2 formation, prompting the attack with intelligent passes and coming through to collect valuable goals with shots that were both accurate and powerful.

Following the shock dismissal of Gullit, the precision and power that he brought to the midfield continued to be important factors under the management of his former team-mate Vialli. He was prominent in the team that won the League Cup and FA Cup and then the 1998 European Cup Winners' Cup. Sadly, Dan was not on the pitch when the final whistle blew to signal a 1-0 victory over Stuttgart. He was never a dirty player, but was sent-off in the closing stages for an innocent-looking challenge that had even the opponents amazed that it was considered worth a red card.

Dan the Man remained a force at the heart of the Chelsea team that battled to the Champions League quarter-finals in 2000. But it was towards the end of that season that he fell out with Vialli after a defeat at Manchester United in April. He stormed

Art Turner
2010

away from Old Trafford before the final whistle after being substituted, and Vialli punished him by never selecting him again – and that included cruelly leaving him out of the squad for the 2000 FA Cup final.

He was shunted off to Bradford for £1 million, then briefly linked up again with Glenn Hoddle at Southampton before returning to his native Romania for the final shots of his eventful career. He has since turned to coaching and management in Romania, Poland and Russia

In his five years at the Bridge, Dan showed that foreign players could settle down and prove their loyalty to the club. He was pure quality and was greatly missed by his army of Chelsea fans.

QUOTE UNQUOTE: Dan Petrescu

"I loved my time at Chelsea, and felt the fans were my friends. They were like an extra man with the way they got behind us during those wonderful cup runs. As long as I live, I will never understand why I was sent-off in the Cup Winners' Cup final. The consolation was that we still won the match. It was a big disappointment the way my Chelsea career ended, but that mustn't cloud the fact that I was generally very happy at the club."

Born: Bouches-du-Rhone, January 22 1968

Career span: 1988-2005

Clubs: Laval (1988-91) Strasbourg (1991-96) Chelsea (1996-2001) 144 League games, 17 goals Marseille (2001-03) Finished his career with Al-Sadd and Al Wakrah in Qatar Total League games: 436, 72 goals

Chelsea honours: FA Cup (1997, 2000) European Cup Winners' Cup (1998) League Cup (1998)

France caps: 50, 5 goals World Cup winner 1998

FRANK was the first of the 'French Foreign Legion' to become a huge favourite at Chelsea when he signed from Strasbourg for £2.5 million in the summer of 1996. He brought instant stability to the defence in his sweeper role that had been performed in earlier seasons by Glenn Hoddle and then Ruud Gullit.

A member of the winning French team in the 1998 World Cup final, he was a big personality who brought a lot of spirit to the dressing-room as well as to the pitch. While a defender of the highest standard, Frank was also a master at springing counter-attacks with perfectly placed long-range passes.

If there was a weakness, it was his lack of authority and power in the air. But he worked on this part of his game so that he was not a weak link when Ruud Gullit – by then manager – decided to scrap the sweeper system and play a more disciplined 4-4-2. Now Leboeuf was expected to play as an orthodox central defender, and he formed a sort of good cop, bad cop partnership with the more rugged and destructive Steve Clarke. Frank – tall, bald, and commanding – was all elegance and panache, while Steve alongside him would dig in with a style that was more familiar to me. But Frank was no pansy, and could unleash a heavy tackle when necessary. His confident manner made him ideal for the job of penalty taker, and Chelsea fans were grateful to him when he scored an extra-time winner from the spot in an FA Cup thriller against Leicester City, with a penalty shoot-out moments away.

At the end of his first season he collected an FA Cup winners' medal, and later teamed-up with Michael Duberry as rock-solid central defenders in the team that added the League Cup and European Cup Winners' Cup to the groaning Chelsea trophy cabinet. It was in that summer of 1998 that he partnered Marcel Desailly in France's stunning World Cup final victory over Brazil in Paris.

He played over 200 games for Chelsea and scored 24 goals – the majority of them from the penalty spot. Frank, popular with the Chelsea faithful, reluctantly moved to

Art Turner 2010

his hometown club Olympique Marseille because he wanted to be close to his dying father. He later wound down his career in Qatar. Always a showman and with bags of charisma, Frank moved to Hollywood where he appeared in several films, played for the Hollywood celebrity soccer team and worked as an interviewer for ESPN.

QUOTE UNQUOTE: Frank Leboeuf

"I am always thankful for what Chelsea brought to my life, I got another dimension because of all that happened to me there. It was a very fulfilling experience. We had a close-knit team and we grew up together, laying the foundation for all the good things that have come since. It was players of the calibre of Gullit, Vialli, Di Matteo, Zola and Mark Hughes who helped make those such amazing years. I still think of Chelsea as my club and if one day I could come back and do something for them I wouldn't think twice about it."

**Born: Accra, Ghana
September 7 1968**

Career span: 1986-2006

**Clubs: Nantes (1986-92)
Marseille (1992-93)
AC Milan (1993-98)
Chelsea (1998-2004)
156 League games, 7 goals
Finished his career with Al-
Gharafa and Qatar
Total League games:
541, 21 goals**

**Chelsea honours: FA Cup
(2000)**

**France caps: 116, 3 goals
World Cup winner 1998
Euro 2000 winner**

MARCEL was close to thirty when he arrived at the Bridge from Milan, and many experts thought he was past his best. He had just won the World Cup with France, and had an exceptional club record behind him. In 1993 he was a Champions League winner with Olympique Marseille and the following year won the trophy again with AC Milan, becoming the first player ever to collect back-to-back Champions League winners' medals. He twice won Italian League titles under the management of Fabio Capello.

Many believed he was burned out when he chose to join Chelsea rather than Manchester United or Liverpool. He proved all the doubters wrong and stayed longer with Chelsea than any of his previous teams and became a hugely respected defender and a captain who inspired by example.

I would loved to have played alongside him, because he was one of those superior players who could only improve the game of those around him, and it was easy to see why he was known as The Rock.

Marcel has a fascinating background. He was born Odenke Abbey in Ghana in 1968 but was given the name Marcel Desailly when his mother married a wealthy French diplomat.

Privately educated, Marcel is an exceptionally intelligent man who upset his father by choosing a career in football rather than in the diplomatic corps.

He was not always a diplomat on the pitch and managed to get himself sent-off in the 1998 World Cup final in which France beat Brazil 3-0. His transfer to Chelsea for £4.6 million in August 1998 astonished the football world and was seen as a statement of intent by the Blues that they were challenging for a permanent place among the world's most powerful clubs.

Marcel got off to shaky start to his Chelsea career, with a defeat at Coventry where he failed to bring two-goal Dion Dublin under control. He learned quickly that the English game was much faster and more physical than in Italy, and he adapted his

style as he fitted in alongside his French international team-mate Frank Leboeuf.

By the end of his first season the Blues had lost just three League games and qualified for the Champions League for the first time, and the following campaign he helped them reach the Champions' League quarter-finals and then win the FA Cup with a victory over Aston Villa in the final, the last one played at the old Wembley.

After he had helped France become Euro 2000 champions, he was in the same month named captain of his country and club. New manager Claudio Ranieri made him Chelsea captain as successor to Dennis Wise and paired him in a defensive partnership with a youngster called John Terry.

Another Frenchman, 23-year-old William Gallas, came in to add to the all-round strength of the side. When injury forced Desailly to take a rest, Gallas dropped in alongside Terry, and they were so effective that he had to fight to get his place back.

Ranieri rotated them throughout the next season which ended with Marcel leading the Blues out in the Millennium Stadium for the 2002 FA Cup final defeat by Arsenal.

Injuries and painful tendonitis troubled Marcel for much of his final seasons at the Bridge, but his powerful and almost imperious presence when fit gave Chelsea a stature that set them apart from lesser teams. He was a major influence on the young John Terry, who has often gone on record saying how much he learned from the master both in how to defend and also skipper a side.

Marcel was there at the start of the Abramovich era. But by then he was having to take third place to the Terry/Gallas pairing and he finally conceded that his Bridge days were over in 2004, the same year in which he played his then record 116th international match for France.

He added another League title medal to his collection when making his final appearances in Qatar. Desailly these days has his fingers in several business pies, has owned a restaurant, is a regular pundit on TV and radio and keeps a close watch on Chelsea and his protégé John Terry. He is currently a UNICEF ambassador to Ghana and often says that the only job that would bring him back to football is manager of the country of his birth. You can bet The Rock would make a great job of it.

QUOTE UNQUOTE: Marcel Desailly

"I got quite a shock when I first joined Chelsea, thinking I could play at the same pace and concentration as when with Milan. But I soon found out that I needed to think quicker and be more physical with my challenges. Frank Leboeuf and I had a good understanding, and then I formed a rewarding partnership with John Terry. I like to think I helped in his development into becoming one of Europe's top defenders. I keep an eye on his progress and I visit Chelsea at every opportunity. The club will always be special to me."

GRAEME had two spells at Chelsea, in between winning a Premier League winners' medal with Blackburn. He was an outstanding left-back who could also play in midfield or on the wing, but his career will mainly be remembered for being clouded by controversies.

He was not your run-of-the-mill footballer, boasting a Masters degree in economics and famously preferring to read the *Guardian* to a tabloid. This led to the sort of dressing-room banter that comes with the territory of being a professional footballer, but it got nasty when rumours spread that Graeme – a married man – was gay.

For much of his career he had to put up with taunts from supporters, and it became a headline-hitting issue when he had an on-pitch bust-up with Liverpool striker Robbie Fowler after the Liverpool striker had made homophobic remarks and gestures.

Despite his success at club and international level, I always got the feeling that Graeme did not really enjoy his days as a professional footballer. It could not have been easy continually having to face crude chants from the fans at all grounds.

Born: Jersey, Channel Islands October 17 1968

Career span: 1987-2005

Clubs: Chelsea (1987-93/1997-2003)
230 League games, 12 goals
Blackburn Rovers (1993-97)
Southampton (2003-05)

Total League games:
403, 20 goals

Chelsea honours: FA Cup (2000) European Cup Winners' Cup (1998) League Cup (1998)

England caps: 36, 1 goal

Spotted by John Hollins while playing youth football in his birthplace of Jersey, Graeme's first spell with Chelsea ended in bitterness. He tore off his shirt and threw it to the ground after being substituted by manager Ian Porterfield. Within a short time he was on his way out of the Bridge and off to Blackburn Rovers in a £700,000 deal in March 1993.

He was a prominent player in Kenny Dalglish's Rovers team that won the Premier League title in 1994-95, but he again made the front pages for the wrong reasons after getting involved in a fist-throwing confrontation with team-mate David Batty during a Champions League tie against Spartak Moscow on November 22 1995.

Four years after selling Le Saux, Chelsea paid out £5 million to buy him back in 1997. This was then a British record fee for a defender. He slipped comfortably back into the Chelsea squad that won the League Cup and Cup Winners' Cup in 1998 and

the FA Cup in 2000, although injuries kept him out of two of the finals.

Twice named in the Professional Footballers' Association Team of the Year (1995 and 1998), he won 36 England caps. These included starting all four England games at the 1998 World Cup finals in France. He scored one international goal against Brazil in 1995, which was later voted the eighteenth greatest goal scored in England's international history. It was a magnificent 30-yard volley, and left us all scratching our heads as to why he did not shoot more often.

Graeme had excellent ball control, an eye for attacking play and a strong tackle. His one major flaw was that he continually made a mess of the final pass when getting into excellent overlapping positions.

He left Chelsea for a second time in 2003, the makeweight in a deal that took him to Southampton in exchange for Wayne Bridge. Graeme decided to call it a day when the Saints were relegated in 2005, and then courted controversy again when he quit the BBCtv punditry team after a row over what he described as broken promises.

QUOTE UNQUOTE: Graeme Le Saux

from his riveting 2007 autobiography, Left Field

"I gravitated towards the couple of foreign lads at the club in my first spell at Chelsea and was called a homosexual. I gravitated towards the foreign lads at the club in my second spell and was called cosmopolitan. The funny thing about my life in football is that, later on, the game began to move towards me. I wasn't an outsider any more. Old-schoolers like Chelsea captains Peter Nicholas and Graham Roberts, who had regarded me as a dork, a swot or a pretentious weirdo, didn't hold sway any more. The men who ruled by intimidation and bullying were marginalised, and a culture that rewarded professionalism took hold."

ROBERTO was a main driving force in the resurgence of Chelsea in the late 1990s after all the scares about going out of business had finally been squashed. From the moment of his first home game against Middlesbrough – scoring the winning goal – he was accepted by the Bridge fans as a true Blue.

It was following a fall-out with his coach at Lazio that Roberto suddenly became available in the transfer market. Manager Ruud Gullit had his ear to the ground and quickly snapped him up for what was then a club record fee of £4.9 million.

It was his precise, positive passing that gave shape and urgency to Chelsea, and his nine goals in his first season included two storming long-range shots against Tottenham and Wimbledon.

Chelsea finished sixth that season, their highest placing since 1989-90, and Roberto made a name for himself in the 1997 FA Cup final with a goal on the run from thirty yards in 42 seconds, then the quickest in Wembley Cup history.

Born: Switzerland May 29 1970
Career span: 1988-2002

Clubs: Schaffhausen (1988-91) FC Zurich (1991-92) Aarau (1992-93) Lazio (1993-96)
Chelsea (1996-2002)
119 League games, 15 goals

Total League games: 323, 31 goals

Chelsea honours: FA Cup (1997, 2000) European Cup Winners' Cup (1998) League Cup (1998)

Italy caps: 44, 2 goals

Manager: MK Dons (2008-09) West Brom (2009-)

In his second season, Roberto found the net ten times and helped lay on many more with his intelligent use of the ball, always putting the correct weight on his passes as Chelsea powered to the Football League Cup and European Cup Winners' Cup. He gave similar service to Italy on his way to 44 caps and two international goals.

Combining perfectly with Gus Poyet, Dennis Wise and Dan Petrescu, Roberto was a main motivator in the 1998-99 season when Chelsea had a run of twenty unbeaten games on the way to third place in the Premier League to qualify for the Champions League.

He overcame injury problems to make a late impact in Chelsea's FA Cup-winning 1999-2000 season, capitalizing on a mistake by Aston Villa goalkeeper David James to score a 71st minute winner in the final.

Disaster struck for Roberto the following season when a triple leg fracture in a

Art Turner
2010

Cup tie against Swiss side St Gallen virtually ended his career. He tried desperately to make a comeback but finally had to admit he was beaten in February 2002 at the age of thirty-one.

In his six years at Chelsea, he made 175 League and Cup appearances and scored 26 goals. He was selected in the squad of Chelsea's greatest ever XI, and the then manager Claudio Ranieri gave him the honour of leading the Chelsea team out for the 2002 FA Cup final. He is now building a new career for himself as a manager, first with MK Dons and then West Bromwich Albion.

QUOTE UNQUOTE: Roberto Di Matteo

"I was very sad when the old Wembley was demolished. It was a lucky place for me, where I enjoyed my happiest moments with Chelsea. They were wonderful times at Stamford Bridge and I had an affinity with the supporters that continues to this day. But it's all history. I now have all my attention on the future as a manager, and I do not have the medals I won with Chelsea on show because I do not wish to live in the past."

EDDIE knew the old Stamford Bridge pitch better than most people. He used to weed it as a thirteen-year-old kid when an associate schoolboy with the club. He later joined the groundstaff and after a loan spell at Cardiff established himself in the first-team squad. He was there for the start of the revolution that laid the foundation for the great club that Chelsea is today.

Glenn Hoddle played a big part in his development from a play-anywhere utility man to a holding midfield player in the Hoddle-devised diamond formation. When Glenn took over as England manager from Terry Venables in 1996, Newton continued to be a vital part of new boss Ruud Gullit's plans.

He had contrasting experiences in his two FA Cup final appearances for Chelsea. In 1994, it was his foul on Ryan Giggs that cost a penalty, which was netted by Eric Cantona to put Manchester United on the way to a thumping 4-0 win. Three years later he scored the second victory-clinching FA Cup final goal against Middlesbrough.

Born: Hammersmith, December 13 1971
Career span: 1990-2000

Clubs: Chelsea (1990-99) 165 League games, 8 goals
Cardiff City (1992 loan)
Birmingham City (1999-2000)
Oxford United (2000) Barnet (2000)
Total League games: 198, 12 goals

Chelsea honours: FA Cup (1997) European Cup Winners' Cup (1998) League Cup (1998)

2 England Under-21 caps

West Bromwich Albion assistant head coach (2009-)

Eddie won the Cup Winners' Cup and League Cup with the club a year later, but was then handicapped by a series of injuries and lost his regular place with the arrival of French World Cup-winning midfielder Didier Deschamps.

He joined Birmingham City in July 1999 on a free transfer before brief spells at various lower league clubs, including Oxford United and Barnet.

Eddie, a convert to Islam, retired due to a knee injury and concentrated on coaching at the Chelsea Academy. He later joined his old team-mate Roberto Di Matteo as assistant coach at MK Dons, and then followed him to West Bromwich Albion in 2009.

QUOTE UNQUOTE: Eddie Newton

"It's amazing what has happened at the Bridge since I was weeding the pitch there as a schoolkid. There will always be a lot of Chelsea blue blood in me because I had my happiest playing days there."

**Born: Paramaribo, Surinam
March 27 1972
Career span: 1990-2008**

**Clubs: Telstar (1990) AZ
Alkmaar (1990-93) SC
Campomaiorense (1995-96)
Boavista (1996-97) Leeds
United (1997-99) Atletico
Madrid (1999-2000)
Chelsea (2000-04)
177 League games, 70 goals
Middlesbrough (2004-06)
Charlton Athletic (2006-07)
Cardiff City (2007-08)**

**Total League games:
468, 197 goals**

**Premier League Golden Boot
winner (1999 – first overseas
winner & 2001)**

Holland caps: 23, 9 goals

JIMMY – or Jerrel to give him his proper name – was a have-boots-will-travel professional who hired himself out as a hit man, and had his most impressive strikes during a four-year stop-off at the Bridge. A muscular and athletic striker, he could hit the ball with awesome power and collected many spectacular goals during his travels.

Born in the South American Republic of Surinam, he began his footballing adventure in the Netherlands with Telstar and AZ Alkmaar, before playing for SC Campomaiorense and Boavista in Portugal on his way to George Graham's Leeds United for £2 million in June 1997.

In his debut season for Leeds he scored 23 goals, and 21 the following year as he helped fire Leeds to a fourth-place finish in the Premier League. His 18 League goals made him the Premier division's joint top scorer.

Jimmy was soon on his travels again this time to Atletico Madrid and with a £12 million price tag. A year – and 24 La Liga goals later – his fee had gone up to £15 million … and it was Chelsea who paid it.

He was an instant hit at the Bridge, scoring 23 goals in 35 league appearances in the 2000-01 season, including a stunning volley from outside the penalty area against Manchester United and a four-goal haul against Coventry City. This time he finished the season out on his own as the Premier League's top marksman, and was the first foreign winner of the Barclays Golden Boot.

For an old former pro like me, it was mind-blowing to see how Chelsea had become all international with players from under many flags. Jimmy teamed up with Iceland's Eidur Gudjohnsen to form one of the most potent striking duos in the League. Together, they hammered in 29 goals in all competitions as Chelsea once again reached the FA Cup final. Jimmy picked up a serious injury in the game before the final and it was obvious he was not completely fit. He was substituted as the Blues went down to a 2-0 defeat against Arsenal. It was during this season when he told Holland he no longer

Art Turner
2010

wanted to be considered for international duty after winning 23 caps.

He was never quite the same force in his last two seasons at the Bridge as a string of injuries took their toll, but he will be remembered for being the club's top scorer three times in four years before he got on his bike yet again, this time travelling to Middlesbrough on a free transfer. By then he had lost half a yard of pace, yet still managed to bang in 23 goals in 58 League games for the Teeside club and helped them reach the Uefa Cup final – going down 4-0 to Sevilla.

Next stop on the Jimmy Floyd Hasselbaink football road was Charlton Athletic, where he got himself into hot water with the authorities after being reported as saying that Chelsea had paid the players an illegal bonus after the 2004 Champions League win over Arsenal. A Premier League inquiry found no evidence to support the claims, which were – surprise, surprise – denied by Chelsea. He netted his first goal for Charlton against, of all teams, Chelsea at Stamford Bridge in September 2006 and got huge applause from the fans for refusing to celebrate the goal.

Jimmy still had surprises in his locker. He moved on to Cardiff, and helped the Welsh club reach the 2007 FA Cup final, losing 1-0 to Harry Redknapp's Portsmouth. One of the few modern players to score more than 300 League and cup goals, this much-travelled footballer has interests in a building company and is now preparing for a new career as a coach and is keen to try his luck as a manager.

QUOTE UNQUOTE: Jimmy Floyd Hasselbaink

"My time playing alongside Eidur was my most exciting in football. We were red hot together, and didn't mind which one of us scored as long as the ball finished in the back of the net. The only disappointing thing about my stay at Chelsea is that we did not win anything, apart from the Charity Shield. I would liked to have been at my peak in the Mourinho years. That would have been quite something."

Born: Kinshasa, Congo (formerly Zaire) February 18 1973

Career span: 1992-present

Clubs: Nantes (1992-97) Marseille (1997-98) Celta Vigo (1998-2000) Real Madrid (2000-03) Chelsea (2003-08) 144 League games, 2 goals Paris Saint-Germain (2008-)

Chelsea honours: Premier League (2005, 2006) FA Cup (2007) League Cup (2005, 2007)

France caps: 71, 0 goals

CLAUDE was the main inspiration of the Chelsea team inherited by Jose Mourinho – a player who seemed to have the stamina and energy of two men. He was brought to the Bridge from Real Madrid for £16.8 million in the summer of 2003 by Claudio Ranieri, who told the press: "He will be the battery of our team."

As he signed for Chelsea, David Beckham took his squad place with Real – leaving the great Zinedine Zidane wondering aloud to the media: "Why bother to put an extra layer of gold paint on our Bentley when the club has sold the entire engine?"

That was how highly Makelele was rated in the game and, in his first season with Chelsea, he helped them finish second in the Premier League and reach the Champions League semi-final.

Following the exit of Ranieri and the entrance of Jose Mourinho, Makelele was a majestic player in Chelsea's successful 2004-05 season as they purred to Premier League and League Cup triumph.

It was his anchoring skills just in front of the back four that inspired the likes of Frank Lampard, Joe Cole, Arjen Robben, Damien Duff, Eidur Gudjohnsen and Didier Drogba to flourish their attacking skills. Makelele's input was recognized by Mourinho, who said at the end of the season, "He is my Player of the Year."

Born in Zaire, Claude moved to Paris when he was a child and followed in his father's footsteps as a professional footballer. He featured with Nantes, Marseille and Celta Vigo before joining *Los Galacticos*, and he was never overshadowed in that star-studded Real Madrid stable. Capped 71 times by France, he was a players' player and rarely got the public praise while helping Real capture two Spanish La Liga titles, the Champions League, the Spanish Super Cup, the European Super Cup and the Intercontinental Cup.

He was the hidden ace in the Real pack, and considered he was undervalued when he discovered he was earning less than half of many of his high profile team-mates.

His request for better terms were rejected and he demanded a transfer, which was when Chelsea captured him. While essentially a defensive holding player, Makelele was also clever at prompting attacks with simple passes to team-mates in threatening positions. Even though into the veteran stage, his energy was a major reason for the Blues capturing two Premier League titles and three domestic cups as Mourinho lived up to his self-billing as the 'Special One'. Makelele later claimed that Mourinho took too much credit and did not give sufficient praise to the players.

At the end of the 2007-08 season and the disappointment of defeat by Manchester United in the Champions League final, Makelele was assumed to be retiring when he returned to France in the middle of a headline-hitting romance with a beautiful French fashion model. But, at the age of 37, he decided to have the last kicks of his career with Paris Saint Germain and in his first season won the French Cup with them.

QUOTE UNQUOTE: Claude Makelele

"Chelsea really fought to get me from Real, and I have a great respect for the club for what they did for me. There were a lot of changes to the team when I joined, many players came and went but we managed to settle down and find not only a team balance but also a team spirit."

Born: Asnieres-sur-Seine, France
August 17 1977

Career span: 1995-present

Clubs: Caen (1995-97)
Marseille (1997-2001)
Chelsea (2001-06)
159 League games, 12 goals
Arsenal (2006-10) Tottenham
Hotspur (2010-)

Chelsea honours: Premier League (2005, 2006) League Cup (2005)

France caps: 84, 5 goals

WILLIAM is considered a Jekyll and Hyde character at Chelsea because of the way he left the Bridge under a black cloud of anger and following bitter arguments with the club officials that could be measured on the Richter scale.

Following his departure for Arsenal in 2006, Chelsea issued a statement that Gallas threatened to deliberately score own goals and get himself sent-off if he was not allowed to leave.

Gallas strongly denied Chelsea's claims and accused the club of "lacking class and hiding behind false accusations."

But regardless of the circumstance of his exit, there is no question that William was one of the most accomplished defenders ever to wear a Chelsea shirt.

Manager Claudio Ranieri bought Gallas from Marseille in May 2001 for £6.2 million with the idea of playing him as a central defender. He developed superb centre-back partnerships with Marcel Desailly and later John Terry. It is part of Chelsea footballing folklore that his partnership with Terry included a run of 16 games without conceding a single goal. He also occasionally played at right-back, but made it clear that he preferred to be in the centre of the defence. His performances in his early days at the Bridge brought him the first of his 84 international caps with France.

Gallas was part of Chelsea's team which won back-to-back Premier League titles and a League Cup under Ranieri's successor Jose Mourinho. The Blues also made the semi-finals of the Champions League that year, but went down 1-0 to Liverpool.

It started to turn sour for William when Mourinho continually played him out of position at full-back, often at left-back even though he is predominantly right-footed.

He came through from the back to steal several vital goals as Chelsea retained their title in 2005-06, including a cracking 25-yard injury-time winner against Tottenham.

His frustration at being played out of position – plus the fact that he did not think he was being paid enough – led Gallas getting into a deadlock over new contract negotiations, and he eventually put in a transfer request that was rejected.

It then got to the point where player and club were exchanging insults and insinuations before – on September 1 2006 – Gallas was transferred to Arsenal as part of the deal that brought Ashley Cole to the Bridge. The Gunners also got £5 million.

Many Chelsea fans turned on Gallas and treated him as a traitor, but the more fair-minded accepted that he had played with style, skill and strength during what were incredibly successful days for the club.

He had a strange time at Arsenal, playing some magnificent football for them and having a long run as captain. But he was involved in more controversy. In February 2008 he staged a one-man sit-down protest at the end of a match at Birmingham in which Arsenal had lost 2-0 and team-mate Eduardo da Silva had suffered a broken leg. This was the moody, brooding, proud genius who had clashed with the Chelsea directors. He was a fierce competitor who hated losing.

Later the same year he fell out with many of his club colleagues when it was reported in the newspapers that he had said his Arsenal team-mates were "not brave enough in the battle".

Gallas claimed his comments had been off the record and had been taken out of context. He has barely spoken to the press since. Arsene Wenger stripped him of the club captaincy.

A month before he lost the captaincy he had been caught by the paparazzi at the wheel of his car, having just left a London nightclub, with a cigarette hanging from his mouth. More bad publicity.

In the summer of 2010 he was the talk of London football again when he joined Tottenham on a free transfer. Arsenal and Chelsea fans will never forgive him.

Born: Abidjan, Ivory Coast March 11 1978 Career span: 1998-present

Clubs: Le Mans (1998-2002) Guingamp (2002-03) Marseille (2003-04) Chelsea (2004-) 169 League games, 88 goals (up to September 11 2010)

Chelsea honours: Premier League (2005, 2006, 2010) FA Cup (2007, 2009, 2010) League Cup (2005, 2007) Premier League and FA Cup double (2010)

Premier League Golden Boot (2007, 2010) African Footballer of the Year (2006, 2009)

Ivory Coast caps: 71, 45 goals

DIDIER is No 1 of all the players in my list that I would least liked to have marked. For a start, he is a magnificent, strong, bullocking nuisance of a centre-forward ... but also one who aggravates opponents by continually going down for what seems no reason at all. I know I would have lost my rag with him and would have been red-carded the moment he tried his falling-over tricks with me.

But when he's on his feet and going for goal, there have been few more dangerous forwards in Chelsea's history. What a powerhouse! He can destroy the tightest defence with a galloping run, either with the ball at his feet or charging in to meet a cross.

He is not all physical strength. He also has subtle touches, and can hit long, raking passes that bring his team-mates into the action. For a bloke who often seems to be feigning injury, he is incredibly brave and dives in where others fear to tread. I just wish he would not go down as if shot when it is clear he has been hardly touched, but I guess that's the modern way.

There was loads of it going on in the 2010 World Cup finals in South Africa where injury prevented Drogba making the sort of impact we expected with his native Ivory Coast team. He is a legend in the land of his birth, and once ended a civil war there by telling the leaders to lay down their arms. They had so much respect for him that they did as he ordered. Wow! You couldn't make that up.

There are few more exciting players to watch than Didier when he is in full flow, and he is fast climbing up the all-time list of Chelsea goalscorers. He has found the net more times than any previous foreign player at the club, and also has many assists with cleverly laid-off passes and with driving decoy runs that carve openings for his colleagues.

Drogba was a late developer, and it was not until he moved from little French club Guingamp to Olympique Marseille for £3.3 million in 2003 that the world began to sit up and take notice of his raw but explosive power.

Chelsea were so impressed that they parted with a record-breaking £24 million

to bring him to the Bridge in 2004. He quickly settled to the pace and demands of the English game and helped Chelsea win their first Premier League title in 2004-05, scoring ten goals and netting a League Cup final goal against Liverpool. He was just warming up. In 2006, he helped Chelsea retain the Premier League title with 12 goals. The following season he won the Barclays Golden Boot as top Premier League marksman with 20 goals, and also scored winning goals in the 2007 League Cup and FA Cup finals.

In 2008, Drogba scored two goals in the Champions League semi-final against Liverpool, which Chelsea won 3-2 at Stamford Bridge. He overtook Peter Osgood as Chelsea's top scorer in European competition, but then got a record he didn't want when sent-off in the 117th minute of the Champions League final for slapping Man United defender Nemanja Vidic. This made him the first outfield player sent-off in a European Cup final. Chelsea lost 6-5 on penalties to United after a 1-1 draw after extra-time. Drogba had been due to take the vital fifth spot-kick in the shootout. Team captain John Terry replaced him and missed after slipping as he took the penalty.

Didier's powerful presence paved the way for Chelsea to break the Manchester United/Arsenal monopoly as he became an FA Cup winner for a second time in 2009, scoring the equaliser in the final against Everton to bring a glorious end to Guus Hiddink's brief reign as manager.

He won a second Golden Boot in 2009-10 as he fired Chelsea to the first League and FA Cup double in their history, collecting 29 goals in the Premier League and netting the only goal in Chelsea's 2010 FA Cup final victory over Portsmouth. His goal against Pompey made him the only player ever to score in six English cup finals.

His fame transcended the football field when he was named one of the world's most influential people by *Time* magazine for his involvement in the peace process that brought an end to the civil war in his homeland.

Drogba was in tears the day Jose Mourinho left the Bridge, and Chelsea fans feared they may lose their great striker. But, despite being linked with half-a-dozen of the world's top clubs, he stayed loyal to the Blues and every goal he scores adds to his growing legend.

He is also making a name for himself away from football as a goodwill ambassador, and he puts action where his mouth is. He donated through the 'Didier Drogba Foundation' his £3 million signing-on fee for his endorsement of Pepsi for the construction of a hospital in his hometown of Abidjan.

Didier is a big man in so many ways. I just wish he wouldn't fall over so easily.

QUOTE UNQUOTE: Didier Drogba

"I was very upset when Jose Mourinho told us that he was leaving. His departure destroyed a certain familiarity we had at the club. Many of us played first and foremost for the manager, but once he departed we had to forget those personal feelings and find another source of motivation."

RICARDO was one of Jose Mourinho's main men, brought by the 'Special One' from his old club Porto after he had looked one of the best centre-backs in the world while playing for Portugal at Euro 2004. He signed for a fee of £19.85 million, and brought instant solidity to the middle of the Chelsea defence alongside home favourite John Terry.

In his debut season, Ricardo helped Chelsea win the Premier League, their first major domestic trophy for more than 50 years and also the less prized League Cup. He and Terry were perfectly balanced, and it was their coolness and control under pressure that was a major factor behind Chelsea repeating their Premier League triumph the following season.

Despite him being a talisman for Mourinho, the two fellow countrymen had a volcanic fall-out at the start of the 2005-06 season when Carvalho criticized the manager's selection policy. He said that Mourinho's decision to drop him for the first game of the season was "incomprehensible".

Born: Amarante, Portugal May 18 1978
Career span: 1997-present

Clubs: FC Porto (1997-2004) Leca (1997-98 loan) Vitoria de Setubal (1999-2000 loan) Alverca (2000-01 loan) Chelsea (2004-2010) 135 League games, 7 goals Real Madrid (2010-)

Chelsea honours: Premier League (2005, 2006, 2010) FA Cup (2007, 2009, 2010) League Cup (2005, 2007) Premier League and FA Cup double (2010)

Chelsea Players' Player of the Year (2007-08)

Portugal caps: 67, 4 goals

The 'Special One' did not hold back with his public response. "Carvalho seems to have problems understanding things." Jose said, "Maybe he should have an IQ test."

He then left him out for the crucial game against Arsenal that Chelsea won 1-0. And just to rub it in that he was the boss, the club hit Ricardo with a reported £85,000 fine (a week's wages).

The two Portuguese men at war soon patched up their quarrel, and Carvalho settled down to become one of the most consistent and competitive central defenders in the Premier League. He was a power in both penalty areas, and in April 2006 he finished off a move he had started deep in his own half by smashing the ball into the Manchester United net to help Chelsea clinch the title for a second consecutive year.

Damaged ligaments meant Carvalho missed the second-leg of the Champions League semi-final against Liverpool, and also the FA Cup final against Manchester United, won for Chelsea with an extra-time goal from Didier Drogba.

His magnificent performances during the 2006-07 season brought him widesprerad praise, including being shortlisted for the Chelsea Players' Player of the Year honour. Carvalho continued his excellent form following the shock departure of Mourinho.

He committed a rare reckless foul in the 2007 Boxing Day match against Aston Villa. His two-footed tackle on Gabriel Agbonlahor earned him a red card. It was completely out of character for him and he issued a public apology.

His solid performances alongside John Terry in the Champions League were instrumental in getting Chelsea through to the final, where they went down 6-5 in a penalty shoot-out with Manchester United in Moscow. Carvalho was voted by his team-mates Chelsea's Players' Player of the Year. Following a recurring knee injury, the sacking of Luiz Felipe Scolari and the arrival of Guus Hiddink, Carvalho lost his place to Brazilian Alex, and a transfer to Inter to link up again with Mourinho fell through. He accused Chelsea of not supporting him during his injury crisis, but he was back in favour when Carlo Ancelotti took over as manager.

Injuries restricted his input to Chelsea's League and FA Cup double season, and in August 2010 he was allowed to team-up again with his old boss Mourinho, this time at Real Madrid who had been trying to sign him on and off for several years. He will always be warmly remembered at the Bridge as one of the finest defenders ever to pull on the blue jersey.

QUOTE UNQUOTE: Ricardo Carvalho

"My last two seasons at Chelsea were something of a nightmare because of one injury after another, but I will always look on the first four years as among my happiest and most satisfying in football. I have had my ups-and-downs with Jose Mourinho but rate him one of the great coaches, and I am delighted to get the chance to play for him for a third time, particularly at Real Madrid, where I have always wanted to test myself."

Born: Romford, June 20 1978
Career span: 1995-present

Clubs: West Ham United (1995-2001) Swansea City (1995-96 loan) Chelsea (2001-present) 323 League games, 106 goals (up to September 11 2010)

Chelsea honours: Premier League (2005, 2006, 2010) FA Cup (2007, 2009, 2010) League Cup (2005, 2007) Premier League and FA Cup double (2010)

FWA Footballer of the Year (2005) FIFA World Player of the Year (runner-up 2005) Chelsea Player of the Year (2004, 2005, 2006)

England caps: 83, 20 goals

I USED to kick Frank Lampard up in the air and he would get up laughing and give me as good as he got. This, of course, was Frank Lampard senior, who was an excellent England left-back with West Ham in the Sixties and all the way through to the Eighties. His son Frank junior has not only followed in his footballing footsteps but has become one of the all-time great midfield players whose scoring record for a non-striker is phenomenal.

Frank Snr and Harry Redknapp were team-mates at Upton Park. They married sisters. The Redknapps produced Jamie and the Lampards Frank Jnr. Some pedigree in that family.

Uncle Harry introduced young Frank to professional football with West Ham, where he was a first-team regular from 1998 after a learning-curve loan spell with Swansea. He was in the Hammers team that featured other outstanding youngsters like Rio Ferdinand and a very young Joe Cole.

Chelsea came calling in 2001 and persuaded the Hammers to part with Frank in return for a cheque for £11 million. He settled into Claudio Ranieri's Blue team as comfortably as if born for the role, and from his debut set a record 164 consecutive Premier League appearances.

In my day, he would have been called an attacking wing-half. In the modern language, he is a box-to-box player, and there is nobody in the world better at getting on the end of movements, picking up the pieces and often planting the ball into the net.

From season one at the Bridge, he has been a prolific goalscorer and was one of the chief driving forces in the team that won back-to-back Premier League titles in 2004-05 and 2005-06 and the domestic cup double in 2007. He was elected Footballer of the Year by the Football Writers' Association in 2005, the oldest individual football award trophy in the world.

His new contract in 2008 was reported to have made him one of the highest paid Premier League footballers, guaranteeing him earnings of £33 million over a period of five years (his £125,000-plus for one week was as much as I earned from wages in

my career! Good luck to him. Wish I could knock off 30-odd years and get stuck into that sort of dosh.

Jose Mourinho, who tried to take him to Inter with him, went on record as saying, "Frank Lampard is the greatest midfield player in the world." His goalscoring record provides plenty of evidence to support the assessment.

The nation got caught up in the emotion of his game and life when, following the death of his mother, he dedicated each goal to her memory, looking up to the sky every time he put the ball into the net. She and his father, Frank Snr, had been his strongest supporters since he first kicked a ball in the garden of the family home in Romford where he was born while his dad was a professional with West Ham.

He was on the scoresheet in the 2008 Champions League final and won the the FA Cup for the second time in 2009, scoring the 72nd minute winning goal in the final against Everton.

The following year he was named the Premier League's Player of the Decade on his way to helping Chelsea capture the Premier League title and FA Cup double. This was his most prolific season to date, scoring 22 League goals and being credited with 17 League assists.

Frank has won the Chelsea Player of the Year award three times and is Chelsea's third all-time goalscorer. He has netted more goals from midfield than any other player in Football League or Premier League history. And he is not just a glory-grabbing goalscorer. He gives 100 per cent to the team effort, and is always involved in the action deep in either half.

His Dad won two England caps, and was as proud as punch when his son followed him as an international, and as I write he is well on his way to collecting a century of caps.

Off the pitch Frank has captured a lot of media interest with his romances, the latest of which is with beautiful television presenter Christine Bleakley. Educated at the independent Brentwood school in Essex, he took an IQ test in which he scored higher than many scientists and intellectuals. At the other extreme, he caused controversy by appearing in a sex video with Rio Ferdinand and Kieron Dyer and unnamed girls.

It seems Frank Lampard Jnr has it all.

QUOTE UNQUOTE: Frank Lampard

"I'm really happy at Chelsea. I had the chance to follow Jose to Inter, but my heart is at the Bridge and I would like to keep going like Ryan Giggs has at Old Trafford. I'm lucky to come from a football family, and so I always got the home support and understanding that is so important. When people ask the secret of my success I say without meaning it as a cliché that it is all down to hard work and giving everything I've got."

**Born: Reykjavik, Iceland
September 15 1978**

Career span: 1995-present

**Clubs: Valur Reykjavik
(1995) PSV Eindhoven (1995-
97) KR Reykjavik (1998)
Bolton Wanderers (1998-
2000)
Chelsea (2000-2006)
182 League games, 54 goals
Barcelona (2006-09) Monaco
(2009-) Tottenham Hotspur
(2010 loan)**

**Chelsea honours: Premier
League (2005, 2006) League
Cup (2005)**

Iceland caps: 61, 24 goals

EIDUR is a Rolls Royce of a player, all silky smooth and with the ability to make or take goals as naturally as an Icelander catching fish. He is the sort of player I used to hate playing against, and you can bet I would have been trying to kick him up in the air back in the days when football was a man's game and physical contact was not a crime.

Some of the tricks he tries on defenders are a pleasure to watch from the stand, but if he had attempted them against me in an earlier life then he would have risked ending up in row Z.

He arrived at Chelsea from Bolton in the summer of 2000, after laying the foundations to his career with his hometown club Valur Reykjavik and PSV of Holland. Gianluca Vialli bought him for a bargain £4 million, but did not get much time to enjoy his prize because he was replaced by Claudio Ranieri two months later.

Ranieri paired him with Dutch striker Jimmy Floyd Hasselbaink and they were dynamite together in the 2001-02 season. The fans used to chant, "If Jimmy doesn't get you then Eidur will." Hasselbaink helped himself to 27 goals and Gudjohnsen chipped in with 23, while playing a supporting role.

The beauty of Gudjohnsen is that he was equally at home for Chelsea as a midfield creator or playing alongside the main target man. His tricky dribbling, sudden acceleration and perfect close-control, combined with deadly finishing, set up 60 assist goals during his five seasons at the Bridge, all that on top of his 54 individual Premier League goals.

His collection included some real crackers, including a spectacular overhead kick against Leeds in 2002-03, a blinder against Fulham the following season and his first professional hat-trick against Blackburn Rovers in 2004. Jose Mourinho knew exactly how to get the best out of him when he took over the reins at the Bridge, and played him to suit any tactical plan, sometimes using him as a central midfielder, occasionally as the holding player, on either wing and sometimes as an out-and-out striker. Jose knew he could rely on him to do the business whatever role he gave him.

The amazing thing is that he was prominent in the Chelsea team throughout what was a secret personal nightmare. He had got himself hooked on gambling, and lost a fortune at the casino tables during his days at the Bridge.

Despite the arrival of an army of high-profile stars, Eidur continued to feature in the Mourinho team and he played a significant part in the 2004-05 Premier League title triumph, scoring 12 goals and making as many with his clever decoy running and precise passes. He also scored in Chelsea's 4-2 win over Barcelona in the 2004-05 Champions League quarter-final. A goal carefully noted by Barca.

Eidur joined the Spanish club in June 2006 as a replacement for Henrik Larsson. The highlight of his stay with Barcelona

was becoming the first Icelander to win the Champions League trophy in 2009, after the Catalans beat Manchester United in the final Rome. He started the following season at Monaco before a spell with Tottenham, Harry Redknapp stealing him from under the noses of his old West Ham club who thought they had signed him. After a season at White Hart Lane, he was on his travels again – this time to Stoke City.

He was born to play the game, and he and his father Arnor created history in 1996 when Eidur made his international debut as a substitute for his father against Estonia. We seem certain to hear more of the Gudjohnsen name in the future. Two of his sons are with the Barcelona academy and drawing interest with their inherited skill.

QUOTE UNQUOTE: Eidur Gudjohnsen

"At whichever club I have played I have always had to compete for my place. It has never been made easy for me. When I arrived at Chelsea they kept saying my position was under threat because of the number of players that were being signed, but I just kept doing my best on the pitch and generally managed to keep a place in the team, probably because of my ability to play well in several positions. I have been through a lot in my career and my life, and have always come out stronger because of the experiences."

**Born: Barking, London
December 7 1980**

Career span: 1998-present

**Clubs: Chelsea (1998-)
312 League games, 19 goals
(up to September 11 2010)
Nottingham Forest (loan
2000)**

**Chelsea honours: Premier
League (2005, 2006, 2010) FA
Cup (2000, 2007, 2009, 2010)
League Cup (2005, 2007)
Premier League and FA Cup
double (2010)**

**PFA Player of the Year (2005)
Chelsea Player of the Year
(2001, 2006)**

England caps: 65, 6 goals

CUT John Terry's wrist and he will bleed Chelsea-blue blood. He is the most successful captain in the club's history and arguably the best and certainly the bravest central defender in the Premier League. He has had to put up with all sorts of private life intrusion by the muck-raking media, but out on the pitch he has never once let down either his club or his country and is rightly idolised by the Bridge faithful.

When he slipped and hit a post with the penalty that cost Chelsea the Champions League final against Manchester United in Moscow in 2008, he openly wept because he felt he was to blame for the defeat. But nobody else had a bad word to say for him because he had the balls to take the penalty in the first place, when others should have volunteered ahead of him. As Frank Lampard said: "JT has not let anybody down. He is a real man's man."

John has been right at the heart of all Chelsea's phenomenal success since an early loan spell at Nottingham Forest helped him find his feet in first-team football. Steve Bruce, then manager at Huddersfield, saw the unknown playing for Forest and bid £750,000 for him. The deal fell through. I wonder what JT's future would have been had he settled for Huddersfield rather than the King's Road?

Brought up in the same Barking area as Bobby Moore on the east side of London, John has been at the Bridge since he was a 14-year-old schoolboy and he grew up fast after getting early lessons in leadership from masters like Marcel Desailly and Frank Leboeuf. They were able to teach him technique and positioning, but what he brought to the table was his own brand of bravery and determination. In my opinion, he would have been an even better player in my day. His physical input would have been applauded in an era when you could tackle without being branded a thug.

It was obvious from the moment he made the breakthrough to the first-team that he was a born defender, and just two seasons after his debut he was voted Chelsea Player of the Year. The fans identified with his 100 per cent commitment to the team effort.

He made the breakthrough to the England team in 2003 and took on the captaincy following the 2006 World Cup, losing the armband in controversial circumstances that

gave the tabloid press a field day. Fabio Capello relieved him of the captaincy after it was revealed that he'd had an affair with the former girlfriend of his ex-Chelsea team-mate Wayne Bridge, who declined to play for England again because he did not want to be in the same dressing-room let alone the same team as JT.

Perhaps John was trying to get his own back on Capello when he publicly questioned the England manager's tactics during the pathetic challenge for the 2010 World Cup. JT thought he was talking for the team but it came across as a one-man revolt. Capello, as if taking off Don Corleone, said: "John Terry, he make-a da beeg mistake." I fully expected him to wake up the next morning to find a decapitated Subbuteo player alongside him in bed.

It was as Chelsea captain that John really thrived. He seemed to grow an extra six inches in the middle of the defence, and led the club to the coveted Premier League title in his first two seasons as skipper. He also lifted the Carling Cup, becoming one of only four Chelsea captains to skipper the club to major honours (I won't say that I am one of them!). He led by example and was voted PFA Player of the Year by his fellow professionals and Chelsea Player of the Year for a second time.

With more than 300 club appearances behind him, he was troubled by a back problem in the 2006-07 season but recovered to become the first captain to lift the FA Cup at the new Wembley. He also had the distinction of scoring the first international goal at the rebuilt stadium.

A succession of injuries limited him to 37 appearances from a possible 62 in 2007-08, yet he made it to Moscow for Chelsea's first Champions League final. Perhaps that was one that he wishes he had missed.

Still worshipped by everybody connected to the club, JT bounced back quickly in 2008-09 to give the team stability as they played musical chairs with the management. Under Luiz Felipe Scolari and then Guus Hiddink, his form never dropped from the sky-high standards he sets for himself.

He produced yet another season of incredible consistency and became the first Chelsea captain to lift the League championship trophy and FA Cup in the same year. Whether playing alongside Ricardo Carvalho, Branislav Ivanovic or Alex, JT was a tower of strength and continually brandishing his fist to demand extra effort from his team-mates. I have rarely seen a better blocker of the ball than John, and if he cannot stop it with his feet he thinks nothing of diving in to put his head and body on the line. He would be the sort of man I would want alongside me in the trenches.

Having lifted his third Premier League trophy, he completed an FA Cup trophy hat-trick in 2010 after overcoming a serious foot injury.

JT has his critics because of some of his behaviour away from football, but nobody can deny that he gives everything he's got for his club and country. I would have loved to have had him as a team-mate in my Chelsea days. He's my kind of man. Yes, a man's man.

QUOTE UNQUOTE: John Terry

"We have the best supporters in the world at Chelsea. Home and away, they give us that extra incentive that can make the difference between winning and losing. Even when I've been getting a tough time from the media they still get behind me, and for that I'll always be grateful. I have never been so heartbroken on a pitch as when I missed the penalty in the Champions League final against Man United. Everybody at the club was sympathetic and supportive, but nothing could ease the pain I felt. I was particularly sorry for all the supporters who had made the trip to Russia."

ASHLEY is one of the finest English-born left-backs of all time, but for a grizzled old pro like me he is too often featured on the gossip rather than the sports pages as part of the so-called celebrity culture.

He has been constantly in the headlines for his private life, while his brilliant football exploits are downplayed. Ash has played more times for England than any other black footballer, is the only player to have won six FA Cup winners' medals and ranks with the best left-sided defenders in the world.

But these footballing feats have all too often been overshadowed by events off the field. His romance, marriage and divorce to pop star Cheryl Tweedy of Girls Aloud filled acres of tabloid front page space, along with allegations of affairs and nightclub drinking sprees.

He arrived at the Bridge from Arsenal in September 2006 under a cloud of suspicion after a long drawn-out saga that finished with him being bought in exchange for William Gallas and a £5 million fee.

He issued a public statement concerning his transfer, declaring that he 'forgave' Arsenal for how he felt he was treated during his time at the North London club that he had joined straight from school. Ash got huge criticism for describing in his autobiography the Arsenal offer of £55,000-a-week as 'a piss take, a paltry offer.' Blimey, a lot of old pros like me never earned that in a year, or five years come to think of it.

When Chelsea next played the Gunners some Arsenal fans waved fake £20 notes in his face after an investigation into his transfer had proved Chelsea illegally tapped him up long before the deal was completed.

Born in London's East End in Stepney, Cole had started his career with Arsenal in 1998. After a brief loan spell with Crystal Palace, he played a total of 228 games for the Gunners, scored nine goals and was a prominent member of the Arsene Wenger side that won two Premier League titles, three FA Cups and a Champions League runners-up medal.

It has been success all the way for Ash. Since joining Chelsea he has collected a

Born: Stepney, London December 20 1980

Career span: 1998-present

Clubs: Arsenal (1998-2006) Crystal Palace (1999-2000 loan) Chelsea (2006-) 114 League games, 6 goals (up to September 11 2010)

Chelsea honours: Premier League (2010) FA Cup (2007, 2009, 2010) League Cup (2007) Premier League and FA Cup double (2010)

Chelsea Players' Player of the Year (2009)

England caps: 83, 0 goals

Art Turner 2010

second Champions League runners-up medal, three more FA Cups and his third Premier League title.

He has a unique and extraordinary collection of medals, but I'm not sure he has enjoyed his success because of the earthquaking events in his private life that have been continually hung out for public scrutiny.

Ash has managed to maintain his high-performance level despite some serious injuries – a damaged knee in January 2007 and a fractured left ankle in February 2010. In the middle of it all he saw off a challenge for his place from Wayne Bridge.

It is his ball control with his left foot, composure when under pressure and a good footballing brain that sets him apart from other defenders. He always uses the ball with purpose, often setting up counter-attacks with his lightning-quick left-wing overlapping raids.

The surprise to me is that he does not score more goals considering how many times he creates space for himself in the opposition half, but he prefers to let his front players take the responsibility for finishing off and provides them with careful passes.

There were rumours that he was unsettled and looking for a move following the departure of Jose Mourinho, who is on record as describing Ashley as "the most talented left-back in the world."

But he knuckled down while battling with crises in his private life, and continued to be a diamond of a player flawed only by off-the-pitch events.

QUOTE UNQUOTE: Ashley Cole

"It's crazy to think I've been playing regularly in the Premier League now for twelve years. The time has simply flown by. There are a few young players coming in now and as one of the senior players I do try to help them but I think I'll leave it mostly to the real leaders in JT, Lamps, Didier – people like that. I am a little too quiet for that sort of leadership. I just concentrate on doing my best on the pitch regardless of what's going on off it."

JOE seems to have been around forever, yet is still in his 20s. Anybody with their ear to the ground in the 1990s knew that there was a sensational young footballer on the rise. He famously scored seven of the eight goals for England against Spain in a youth international, and Manchester United were reported as being ready to part with £10 million for him when he was a 16-year-old apprentice with West Ham.

It was the then Hammers manager Harry Redknapp who brought him along as a youngster at Upton Park, and was quoted as saying: "He is the most naturally gifted player I've ever clapped eyes on, and is years ahead in his head of other young footballers."

Young Joe suddenly felt lost when his mentor Harry moved on, and he went off the boil for a while until new manager Glenn Roeder woke the genius in him by handing him the West Ham captaincy at just 21. He could not stop the Hammers from going down in 2003, and this was when Chelsea moved in to save him for the Premier League where he belonged.

They had just become awash with the money of Russian billionaire Roman Abramovich, and agreed to pay West Ham £6.6 million for Joe's skilled services. It took Chelsea's pre-season spending to £43 million as he joined Damien Duff, Geremi, Wayne Bridge, Arjen Robben and Glen Johnson at the Bridge.

Equally brilliant in the middle of the park or on the wings, Joe's strength was his ability to unlock defences with quick, incisive passes and then taking the return ball and making explosive bursts that caught defenders napping.

He did not show his true form at Chelsea until the arrival of Jose Mourinho, who immediately knew how to get the best out of Joe as a supporting player to the main strikers. Joe was often used as a motivating substitute as Chelsea became a dominant force when they won three Premier League titles and two FA Cups. He would have made a greater impact but for a long lay-off following a stress fracture of the foot.

Watching from the sidelines, I got the impression that Joe never felt fully integrated into the Chelsea team and it came as no surprise to me when he decided to cash in on

Born: Paddington, London November 8 1981

Career span: 1998-present

Clubs: West Ham United (1998-2003)
Chelsea (2003-10)
183 League games, 28 goals
Liverpool (2010-)

Chelsea honours: Premier League (2005, 2006, 2010)
FA Cup (2007, 2009, 2010)
League Cup (2005, 2007)
Premier League and FA Cup double (2010)

Chelsea Player of the Year (2008)

England caps: 56, 10 goals

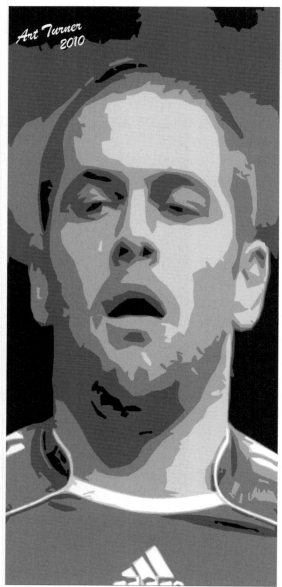
Art Turner
2010

his talent the moment he became a free agent under the Bosman ruling, which meant he could move anywhere without a fee.

There were a queue of clubs jostling for his services, and he seemed set to join his old mentor Harry Redknapp at Spurs until Liverpool moved in and agreed to his £90,000-a-week wage conditions.

He got off to a miserable start to his Anfield career – getting red-carded in his debut for a challenge out on the touchline that was not his style at all, and then missing a penalty in his next match

But he has too much talent to be anything but a success at Liverpool, provided manager Roy Hodgson uses him in the way that Mourinho did, prompting and inspiring the attack just behind the front men.

Along with everybody else, I could not understand why Fabio Cappello did not make more use of his skills at the 2010 World Cup finals. I think that perhaps John Terry's demands that he should be used to unlock defences went against him. Fabio made it clear that he and not JT was picking the team.

But there will be more caps to come. 'Boy Wonder' Joe has grown up now, and is ready to take the responsibility of leading rather than following.

QUOTE UNQUOTE: Joe Cole

"It was not easy deciding to leave Chelsea after some wonderful years. But I think I needed the challenge of a new club, and I was delighted that Liverpool came in for me. When I am an old man, I look forward to telling my grandkids about the great days I had at Stamford Bridge – where the supporters are second-to-none. For me, the most memorable times were when Jose Mourinho was in charge. He made everything seem exciting."

PETR is a challenger to Manchester United's Peter Schmeichel for the title of greatest foreign goalkeeper to play in the Premier League. He has been consistently outstanding for Chelsea since joining them from French club Rennes in 2004.

He is something of a miracle man, because it was feared his career was finished following a serious head injury against Reading in October 2006. Royals' winger Stephen Hunt challenged for the ball inside Chelsea's penalty area in the first minute of a League match at the Madejski Stadium, and Cech was knocked unconscious as Hunt's knee hit his head (remarkably, his deputy Carlo Cudicini was knocked-out in the same match and John Terry ended up in goal).

Cech underwent life-saving surgery for a depressed skull fracture, and manager Jose Mourinho stormed: "The challenge was a disgrace. Petr is lucky still to be alive."

It was later revealed that Cech has an abnormally weak skull caused by the fact that he is one of triplets.

When he made his comeback against Liverpool in January 2007, he was wearing a uniquely designed headguard made by a company in New Zealand that specialise in manufacturing protective rugby gear.

The headguard has become the Cech trademark, and it is expected that other goalkeepers will eventually wear one to avoid head injuries. Blimey, they would need suits of armour if they played in the good old bad old days when goalkeepers used to get battered by powerhouse forwards like Ted Drake, Nat Lofthouse and Bobby Smith.

Chelsea snapped up Cech after he was voted into the Euro 2004 all-star team. He was chiefly responsible for the Czech Republic reaching the semi-finals.

Petr had laid the foundations to his career with his hometown club Pizen, then FK Chmel Blsany and Sparta Prague. Arsenal wanted to buy him but could not get a work permit, so Petr moved to France with Rennes.

Born: Pizen, Czech Republic May 20 1982
Career span: 1999-present

Clubs: FK Chmel Blsany (1999-2001) Sparta Prague (2001-02) Rennes (2002-04) Chelsea (2004-)
187 League games (up to September 11 2010)

Chelsea honours: Premier League (2005, 2006, 2010) FA Cup (2007, 2009, 2010) League Cup (2005, 2007) Premier League and FA Cup double (2010)

Premier League Golden Glove (2005, 2010)

Czech Republic caps: 70

Art Turner
2010

It was Claudio Ranieri who brought him to the Bridge for a bargain £3.5 million as an understudy to Cudicini, but he quickly proved he was more reliable and consistent than the unpredictable Italian.

He currently holds the Premier League record for fewest appearances required to reach 100 clean sheets, achieving the target in just 180 League games. He also holds a Czech record of having gone 928 minutes unbeaten in all competitions in 2001-02. During the 2004-05 season, Petr went 1,025 minutes without conceding a goal, a Premier League best until beaten by Edwin van der Sar for Manchester United. Petr was given a special award in 2004-05 for keeping an incredible 25 clean sheets. He has won the Barclays Premier League Golden Glove twice, and was voted Best Champions League goalie in 2005, 2007 and 2008. They say he is a nuisance when going into hotels because he always demands clean sheets. Well, I thought it was funny.

Petr's strengths are good reflexes, excellent positional sense and catching ability almost in the Catty Bonetti class. He is never afraid to boss his goal area, and he has a well-grounded understanding with John Terry as to when the call is his. His very presence spreads calm and confidence to the players in front of him.

He got caught up in a public row with former manager Luiz Felipe Scolari, who accused Cech, Michael Ballack and Didier Drogba of causing his sacking, saying that they "did not accept my training methods or my demands".

Scolari claimed that the start of the rebellion stemmed from a row between he and Cech over the choice of goalkeeper coach. Petr strongly denied the accusation, saying that he was "disappointed with Scolari because never in my life have I had a personal goalkeeping coach".

He saved a penalty against Portsmouth in the 2010 FA Cup final to ensure that Chelsea completed the League and FA Cup double for the first time in their history.

Petr, an articulate and intelligent man, is proud of his Czech nationality and made sure his two children were born in Prague. The fans at the Bridge love him, and always give him loud applause the moment he arrives on the goal line. There have been few, if any, better goalies to stand between the Chelsea posts.

QUOTE UNQUOTE: Petr Cech

"I was appreciative of Chelsea's concern and support following my head injury, and the fans were unbelievable in the way they got behind me when I came back into the team. There has been outside criticism because I continue to wear the headguard, but these comments are made by ignorant people who do not understand that I am following medical orders to keep wearing it. Believe me, I would love to play without it but I consider it sensible to do what the medical experts suggest."

CHOPPER'S CHELSEA: 50. Michael Essien

Born: Accra, Ghana December 3 1982

Career span: 2000-present

Clubs: Bastia (2000-03) Lyon (2003-05) Chelsea (2005-) 119 League games, 14 goals (up to September 11 2010)

Chelsea honours: Premier League (2006, 2010) FA Cup (2007, 2009, 2010) League Cup (2007) Premier League and FA Cup double (2010)

Chelsea Player of the Year (2007) BBC African Footballer of the Year (2006)

Ghana caps: 51, 9 goals

LAST – but certainly not least – in the top 50 Chelsea players of my lifetime comes Michael Essien, a fabulous player with hardly a weakness in his game. It has been heartbreaking for me having to leave out many players that I rate highly, but I had no doubts about putting Michael into my Chopper's Chelsea list.

Essien is a manager's dream. He can play anywhere, run all day, score or stop goals and can hold on to the ball or release it with total accuracy. And he's got a tackle that can be very meaty. Possibly his ability to take multiple roles has stopped him being identified as an exceptional individualist in his own right but, as team players go, they do not come better or more effective. He does not hold back with his challenges, and has collected yellow cards like confetti and the occasional red, although he is never a deliberately dirty player.

He arrived at the Bridge in August 2005 when Chelsea agreed a club record £26 million fee for the Ghanaian, finally ending a long-running transfer saga that was later at the centre of an official inquiry.

Born in the same Ghana territory as Marcel Desailly, he is legend in his homeland where he is nicknamed 'The Bison' because of his strength and stamina. He plays boss-man central midfielder for Ghana, and we all wonder how the already impressive Black Stars would have fared at the 2010 World Cup had he not been out injured.

As well as being a midfield anchorman or creator, Essien also pops up with vital goals – often of the spectacular variety. His late, dramatic equaliser against Arsenal in December 2006 was voted Chelsea's Goal of the Season, and was closely contested by an explosive run finished by an angled drive into the Valencia net that sent the Blues into the 2007 Champions League semi-final.

His ability was noted beyond British shores. He was nominated for the prestigious FIFA World Player of the Year award three years in succession. And also got three consecutive nominations for the coveted Ballon d'Or. He is always highly placed in the African Player of the Year awards.

Michael never forgets his roots and, in December 2009, he launched the Michael

Essien Foundation (MEF) in his home city of Accra, which will be aimed at helping the poor. In July 2010 this fine example of a footballing hero was appointed a Peace Ambassador by the African Union.

A succession of injuries have stopped him making an even bigger impact on the world stage, but he has achieved enough already to be recognized as one of Chelsea's all-time greats.

QUOTE UNQUOTE: Michael Essien

"Joining Chelsea did wonders for my confidence, and I was able to grow both as a player and as a man. I admit to being aggressive on the football field. That is because it is a very competitive game and I like to try to assert myself, but I never deliberately go out to hurt an opponent. I am so grateful for the support I have received from the fans at Stamford Bridge. They always make me feel at home, and in return I try to do my best for the team."

CHELSEA
V.
CHELSKI

Now for some fun. See if you agree with my selection of an all-British Chelsea side to face a team of Chelsea foreigners.

THE RULES:

You can only pick the British players from those named in my list, which rules out masters such as Glenn Hoddle and Mark Hughes.

For the foreign team, you can pick any overseas player provided he spent at least a season at The Bridge.

The formations must be 4-4-2, so for each side you want a goalkeeper, two full-backs, two central defenders, four midfield players that can include wingers and two out-and-out strikers.

Then select a British manager from Stamford Bridge bosses for the Chelsea team, and an overseas manager for Chelski

One more rule ... I am taking the liberty of picking myself for the British Chelsea team. It's my book, so I'll do what I want :-) If you want to pick an argument, I'll see you behind the Shed ...

THE GOALKEEPERS

THIS was the easiest choice of all, for both teams. There could be only one selection for the British Chelsea team, **Peter 'The Cat' Bonetti.** We played together hundreds of times and I could count his bad games on the fingers of a one-armed bandit. I have seen few goalkeepers to match him for catching a ball and, the few times he took up wrong positions, he was quick and agile enough to get himself out of trouble. He was athletic and brave, and a reliable team-mate. I felt choked for him when he was blamed for England's World Cup defeat against West Germany at the 1970 World Cup. He was pitched into the game at the last minute and was totally lacking in match practice. He took the stick from the press and public like a man, and had the character to return to our goal-line and play as well as ever, and at the end of the following season he played a major part in helping us win the European Cup Winners' Cup.

My choice for Chelski is the consistent and brave **Petr Cech**. When he got that head injury at Reading, I was one of the many old pros who reckoned he would never be the same again. It was the sort of terrible blow that we were convinced would shatter his confidence in a position in which self-belief plays a huge part in performances. He has proved all the doubters wrong in a big way, playing better than ever since recovering from the injury, spreading calm to the defence with his defiant displays. He saw off the challenge of the sometimes unpredictable Carlo Cudicini, and settled down to perform wonders at the back of the defence, where he had an all-important understanding with his central defenders. His powers of concentration are remarkable, which explains why he has kept so many blank sheets. There has been silly criticism of him because he continues to wear protective head gear, but if it gives him confidence then he would be a fool not to wear it.

THE BACK LINE DEFENDERS

I HAD no hesitation in picking **Ken Shellito** as my right-back in the British Chelsea defence. He was lightning-fast, had a strong tackle and good distribution. He would have established himself as one of England's greatest full-backs but for injury bringing an early end to his career. Left-back gave me a headache, but I finally had to give the nod to the extremely gifted **Ashley Cole** over my old team-mate Eddie McCreadie, who was one of the finest left-backs of the 1960s and early 70s. I picked myself for the number six shirt alongside **John Terry**, and reluctantly allow him the captain's armband. He is a born leader and I would have loved the chance to play alongside him. JT is a dominating and decisive player, who believes, like me, that you should not take prisoners when the going gets tough. The Chelski forwards would certainly feel our presence!

My Chelski full-backs are **Branislav Ivanovic** and **Celestine Babayaro**, both good footballing defenders who play with their heads as well as their feet. I thought about Australian-born Tony Dorigo for the Number 3 shirt, but decided on Babayaro because he was the better all-round player. The central defenders would be the magnificent **Marcel Desailly** and the strong and solid **Ricardo Carvalho**. I also considered finding places for Frank Leboeuf, William Gallas and Dan Petrescu, but was happy with the balance of the back line. Petrescu often played at full-back but could not tackle his way out of a paper bag, and was better suited to a midfield role. This team would be certain to play football from the back, because each of the players is comfortable on the ball and equipped to start counter-attacks with well-placed clearances. Babayaro was only just outside my Top 50 list, but I would order him to cut out those amazing flip-somersaults when he scores and save his energy for the game.

Celestine Babayaro, who narrowly missed a place in Chopper's Top 50 list

THE MIDDLE FOUR

THE midfield quartet for my British Chelsea is dripping with individual skill and class. Think of these four artists playing together and I am sure you will lick your lips in anticipation: **Alan Hudson**, **Charlie Cooke**, **Frank Lampard** and **Joe Cole**. Each one of them a complete master of the ball. I can hear you saying, 'But who will win the ball?' Well I will happily come forward from the heart of the defence to collect the ball – by force, if necessary – and I will then immediately release it to one of these geniuses to use their creative skill or, in the case of Lamps, his awesome running power. I preferred the dribbling of Charlie Cooke to the measured passes of Terry Venables and Ray Wilkins, because I have Alan Hudson doing the conducting job for me. Frank Lampard kept John Hollins out because of his extraordinary goalscoring record, and Dennis Wise lost out to Joe Cole's better ball control.

What a battle for supremacy it would be in midfield when you see my Chelski middle four: **Michael Essien**, **Gianfranco Zola**, **Ruud Gullit** and **Claude Makelele**. Zola and Gullit together would be about as good a midfield combination as you could find anywhere in the world, and there have been few better all-round players wearing a Chelsea shirt than Michael Essien. He is phenomenal. There would be no worries here about who would challenge for the ball. Makelele is a master at winning the ball and then holding it, while patrolling just in front of the back line of defenders. He would then relay the ball to Zola or Gullit, who together would have the ability to take any defence apart. Gullit did not play enough games for Chelsea to get into my Top 50, but had he passed the 150-mark he would have walked into my list. He would be a challenger for a place in any top ten all-time list.

THE TWIN STRIKERS

HOW about this for a dream pairing: **Jimmy Greaves** and **Peter Osgood**! Two of Chelsea's favourite sons playing together at the head of the attack would provide fun for the spectators and nightmares for the opposition. I have not seen a more positive or prolific goal scorer than Greavsie when he was just a kid at Chelsea, and Ossie had more natural talent than any footballer I ever played with. I was sad not to be able to find room for Bobby Tambling and Ian Hutchinson. Can you imagine what Greavsie and Ossie would cost together in today's transfer market? Let the bidding start at 100 million quid.

For Chelski I have combined the talents of **Didier Drogba** and **Gianluca Vialli,** who, between them, have taken the art of goalscoring to a new high. In reserve I have Jimmy Floyd Hasselbaink, Eidur Gudjohnsen and Arjen Robben. The raw power of Drogba and the guile of Vialli would make life tough for the British Chelsea defence and I am now beginning to wonder if perhaps I would be better off on the bench!

Gianluca Vialli

BRITISH CHELSEA

PETER BONETTI

KEN SHELLITO   JOHN TERRY   RON HARRIS   ASHLEY COLE

ALAN HUDSON   FRANK LAMPARD   CHARLIE COOKE   JOE COLE

JIMMY GREAVES   PETER OSGOOD

CHELSKI

PETR CECH

IVANOVIC   MARCEL DESAILLY   RICARDO CARVALHO   CELESTINE BABAYARO

MICHAEL ESSIEN   CLAUDE MAKELELE   GIANFRANCO ZOLA   RUUD GULLIT

DIDIER DROGBA   GIANLUCA VIALLI

I will make my fondly remembered old bosses Tommy Docherty and Dave Sexton joint managers of the British team, and I guess there can only be one manager of Chelski. It has to be the 'Special One,' Jose Mourinho. Whatever you think of him, nobody can argue with his extraordinary achievements while in the Chelsea hot seat.
Now sit back and enjoy the game in your imagination. It can only be a classic.
I'll guess at a 4-4 draw. Thanks for your company. Now for the records ...

CHOPPER'S CHELSEA: For the Record

I get annoyed when I buy a sports book and find the statistics are plonked at the back in tiny type so that you can hardly read the facts and figures. Well this book is going to be different. I am giving the records the platform they deserve.

I have asked sports statistician **Michael Giller** to produce a full list of Chelsea records in easy to read style, so that the teams and players that created them get the projection that they warrant. It turns my book into a treasure chest of information.

Please note that all the records are correct up to September 11 2010. This book is being sent to the printers just after Chelsea have started the new season with three Premier League wins including two 6-0 victories!

I just wonder if the sports records section is going to need to be rewritten by the time the shooting and the shouting is over in the 2010-11 season.

One record not featured is the one on which I sang with the rest of the lads back in 1972 – *Blue is the Colour,* which went to No 5 in the pop charts. Just for the record, this was our choir: Tommy Baldwin, Peter Bonetti, Charlie Cooke, John Dempsey, Marvin Hinton, John Hollins, Peter Houseman, Alan Hudson, Steve Kember, Eddie McCreadie, Paddy Mulligan, Peter Osgood, David Webb and me! Enjoy the following records and thanks for your company in what, I think you will agree, is a very select book!

Most in total:
Ron Harris (1961-80) **795**

Most in League:
Ron Harris (1961-80) **655**

Most in FA Cup
Ron Harris (1961-80) **64**

Most in League Cup
Equal: **Ron Harris** (1961-80)
John Hollins (1963-75/1983-84) **48**

Most in FA Cup
Ron Harris (1961-80) **64**

Most in European competition
Frank Lampard (2001-present) **80**

John Hollins, most consecutive games

Most consecutive
John Hollins (Aug. 1971 to Sept. 1974) **167**

Most Consecutive in the League
Frank Lampard (Oct. 2001 to Dec. 2005) **164**

Most games in a single season
Frank Lampard (2006-07) **62**

This is the Top 10 Chelsea table for club appearances in all post-war competitions

		Years	Total
1	Ron Harris	1961–1980	795
2	Peter Bonetti	1959–1979	729
3	John Hollins	1963–75/83–84	592
4	Frank Lampard	2001–present	482
5	John Terry	1998–present	462
6	Dennis Wise	1990–2001	445
7	Steve Clarke	1987–1998	421
8	Kerry Dixon	1983–1992	420
9	Eddie McCreadie	1962–1974	410
10	John Bumstead	1976–1991	409

*Figures correct as at September 11 2010

Roy Bentley, the first Chelsea player to appear in the World Cup finals

Most capped England player
Frank Lampard, 81 while at Chelsea, 2 with West Ham **83** in total

First Chelsea player to play for England
George Hilsdon v Northern Ireland, 16 February 1907

First Chelsea player to play for England in the World Cup finals
Roy Bentley v. Chile, Rio de Janeiro 25 June 1950

First foreign (non-UK) player to appear for Chelsea
Nils Middelboe (Denmark)
The legendary Danish Olympic star made his debut v. Derby County at the Bridge on 15 November 1913. Known as the Great Dane because of his height (6ft 2in), he played 175 games for the Blues up until 1923, after which he became an international referee

First black player
Paul Canoville 12 April 1982 v. Crystal Palace

Youngest player
Ian 'Chico' Hamilton 16 years 138 days, v. Tottenham, 18 March 1967

Oldest player
Dick Spence 39 years 57 days, v. Bolton Wanderers, 13 September 1947

First substitute
John Boyle, replacing George Graham v. Fulham, 28 August 1965

Youngest captain
Ray 'Butch' Wilkins, eighteen when manager Eddie McCreadie handed him the captaincy in 1975 in succession to the previous youngest skipper Ron Harris (22)

Most goals in total
Bobby Tambling 202 (1959-70)

Most goals in a season
Jimmy Greaves 43 (First Division 1960-61)

Most goals in one match
George Hilsdon 6 v. Worksop, FA Cup, First Round, 11 January 1908

Most League goals in total
Bobby Tambling 164 (1959-70)

Most League goals in a season
Jimmy Greaves 41 (First Division, 1960-61)

Most League goals in one match **5**
George Hilsdon v. Glossop, Second Division, 1 September 1906
Jimmy Greaves v. Wolves, First Division, 30 August 1958
Jimmy Greaves v. Preston North End, First Division, 19 December 1959
Jimmy Greaves v. WBA, First Division, 3 December 1960
Bobby Tambling v. Aston Villa, First Division, 17 September 1966
Gordon Durie v. Walsall, Second Division, 4 February 1989

Jimmy Greaves' most prolific goalscoring season was with Chelsea in 1956-57, while still an apprentice professional. He scored **114** goals and Chelsea presented him with an illuminated address to mark the feat. On the first day of the following season he made his League debut and scored for Chelsea against Spurs at White Hart Lane. It was the start of the great goal rush.

Jimmy Greaves was captain for the day in his final appearance for Chelsea against Nottingham Forest at the Bridge in 1961 ... and signed off with a four-goal blast

Most Premier League goals in total
Frank Lampard 106 and counting (2001-)

Most Premier League goals in a season
Didier Drogba 29 (2009-10)

Most Premier League goals in one match **4**
Gianluca Vialli v. Barnsley, Premier League, 24 August 1997
Jimmy Floyd Hasselbaink v. Coventry, Premier League, 21 Oct. 2000
Frank Lampard v. Derby County, Premier League, 12 March 2008
Frank Lampard v. Aston Villa, Premier League, 27 March 2010

Most FA Cup goals in total
Bobby Tambling 25 (1959-70)

Most FA Cup goals in a season
Peter Osgood 8 (1969-70)

Most FA Cup goals in one match
George Hilsdon 6 v. Worksop, FA Cup, First Round, 11 January 1908

Most FA Cup final goals in total
Didier Drogba 3 (v Man U 2007, v Everton 2008, v Portsmouth 2010)

Most League Cup goals in total
Kerry Dixon 25 (1983-92)

Chelsea striker Kerry Dixon, who had a one-man war on the League Cup

Most League Cup goals in a season
Kerry Dixon 8 (1984-85)

Most League Cup goals in one match
Kerry Dixon 4 v. Gillingham, League Cup, 13 September 1983

Most League Cup final goals in aggregate
Didier Drogba 4 (v Liverpool 2005, v Arsenal (2), 2007, v Spurs 2008)

Most Cup final goals in aggregate
Didier Drogba 7 (3 FA Cup, 4 Football League Cup)

Most goals in one final
David Speedie 3 v. Manchester City, Full Members Cup, 23 March 1986

Most European goals in total
Didier Drogba 26 (2004-)
Most European goals in a season
Tore Andre Flo 8 (UEFA Champions League, 1999-00)

Most European goals in one match:
Peter Osgood 5 v. Jeunesse Hautcharage, European Cup Winners' Cup, First Round, Second Leg, 29 September 1971

Most hat-tricks
Jimmy Greaves 13 (1957-61)
Most penalties scored
Dick Spence 40 (1934-50)

Most international goals
Didier Drogba 36 for the Ivory Coast (45 in total)

Oldest goalscorer
Dick Spence 38 years 282 days v. Wolves, First Divi, 26 April 1947
Youngest goalscorer
Ian Hamilton 16 years 138 days v. Spurs, First Div., 18 March 1967

Fastest goalscorer: **12** seconds
Keith Weller v. Middlesbrough, Football League Cup, 7 October 1970

This is the Top 10 Chelsea table for club goalscorers in all competitions

		Years	Total
1	Bobby Tambling	1959–1970	202
2	Kerry Dixon	1983–1992	193
3	Frank Lampard	2001–present	158
4	Roy Bentley	1948–1956	150
5	Peter Osgood	1964–74/78–79	150
6	Didier Drogba	2004–present	135
7	Jimmy Greaves	1957–1961	132
8	George Mills	1929–1943	125
9	George Hilsdon	1906–1912	108
10	Barry Bridges	1958–1966	93

*Figures correct as at September 11 2010

Season by season, the top post-war marksmen

Season			Goals
1946-47	Tommy Lawton	First Division	26
1947-48	Armstrong/Campbell	First Division	11
1948-49	Roy Bentley	First Division	20
1949-50	Bentley/Billington	First Division	17
1950-51	Roy Bentley	First Division	8
1951-52	Bentley/D'Arcy	First Division	12
1952-53	Roy Bentley	First Division	12
1953-54	Roy Bentley	First Division	21
1954-55	Roy Bentley	First Division	21
1955-56	Roy Bentley	First Division	14
1956-57	McNichol/Tindall	First Division	10
1957-58	Jimmy Greaves	First Division	22
1958-59	Jimmy Greaves	First Division	32
1959-60	Jimmy Greaves	First Division	29
1960-61	Jimmy Greaves	First Division	41
1961-62	Bobby Tambling	First Division	20
1962-63	Bobby Tambling	Second Division	35
1963-64	Bobby Tambling	First Division	17
1964-65	Barry Bridges	First Division	20
1965-66	George Graham	First Division	17
1966-67	Bobby Tambling	First Division	21
1967-68	Peter Osgood	First Division	16
1968-69	Bobby Tambling	First Division	17
1969-70	Peter Osgood	First Division	23
1970-71	Keith Weller	First Division	13

Season	Player	Division	Goals
1971-72	Peter Osgood	First Division	18
1972-73	Garland/Osgood	First Division	11
1973-74	Tommy Baldwin	First Division	9
1974-75	Ian Hutchinson	First Division	7
1975-76	Ray Wilkins	Second Division	11
1976-77	Steve Finnieston	Second Division	24
1977-78	Tommy Langley	First Division	11
1978-79	Tommy Langley	First Division	15
1979-80	Clive Walker	Second Division	13
1980-81	Colin Lee	Second Division	15
1981-82	Clive Walker	Second Division	16
1982-83	Mike Fillery	Second Division	9
1983-84	Kerry Dixon	Second Division	28
1984-85	Kerry Dixon	First Division	24
1985-86	Dixon/Speedie	First Division	14
1986-87	Kerry Dixon	First Division	10
1987-88	Gordon Durie	First Division	12
1988-89	Kerry Dixon	Second Division	25
1989-90	Kerry Dixon	First Division	20
1990-91	Gordon Durie	First Division	12
1991-92	Dennis Wise	First Division	10
1992-93	Harford/Stuart	Premier League	9
1993-94	Mark Stein	Premier League	13
1994-95	John Spencer	Premier League	11
1995-96	John Spencer	Premier League	13
1996-97	Gianluca Vialli	Premier League	9
1997-98	Flo/Vialli	Premier League	11
1998-99	Gianfranco Zola	Premier League	13

Nicolas Anelka was leading Chelsea marksman in the Premier League in 2008-09

1999-00	Poyet/Flo	Premier League	10
2000-01	J. Floyd Hasselbaink	Premier League	23
2001-02	J. Floyd Hasselbaink	Premier League	23
2002-03	Gianfranco Zola	Premier League	14
2003-04	J. Floyd Hasselbaink	Premier League	13
2004-05	Frank Lampard	Premier League	13
2005-06	Frank Lampard	Premier League	16
2006-07	Didier Drogba	Premier League	20
2007-08	Frank Lampard	Premier League	10
2008-09	Nicolas Anelka	Premier League	19
2009-10	Didier Drogba	Premier League	29

STAMFORD BRIDGE

Attendance	Opponents	Competition	Date
100,000	Dynamo Moscow	Friendly	November 13, 1945
82,905	Arsenal	First Division	October 12, 1935
77,952	Swindon Town	FA Cup	April 13, 1911
77,696	Blackpool	First Division	October 16, 1948
76,000	Tottenham	First Division	October 16, 1920
75,952	Arsenal	First Division	October 9, 1937
75,043	Wolves	First Division	April 9, 1955
74,667	Arsenal	First Division	November 29,1955
74,365	Birmingham City	FA Cup	March 4, 1931
72,614	Arsenal	First Division	April 3, 1953

WEMBLEY STADIUM

Attendance	Opponents	Competition	Venue	Date
100,000	Leeds United	FA Cup final	Wembley	April 11, 1970
100,000	Stoke City	League Cup final	Wembley	March 4, 1972
100,000	Tottenham	FA Cup final	Wembley	May 20, 1967
90,000	Millwall	War Cup South final	Wembley	April 7, 1945
89,826	Man United	FA Cup final	Wembley	May 19, 2007
89,391	Everton	FA Cup final	Wembley	May 30, 2009
88,335	Portsmouth	FA Cup final	Wembley	May 15, 2010
88,103	Arsenal	FA Cup semi-final	Wembley	April 18, 2009
87,660	Tottenham	League Cup final	Wembley	Feb. 24, 2008
85,896	Man United	Community Shield	Wembley	August 9, 2009

THE NET BUSTERS

All-time biggest win
13-0
v. Jeunesse Hautcharage, Cup Winners' Cup, 1st Round 2nd Leg, 29 September 1971

Record League win
8-0 v. Wigan Athletic, FA Premier League, 9 May 2010

Record FA Cup win
9-1 v. Worksop Town, Round 1, 11 January 1908

Record League Cup win
7-0 v. Doncaster Rovers, Round 3, 16 November 1960

Longest sequence of League wins
11 25 April 2009 to 20 September 2009

Longest sequence without a League win
21 3 November 1987 - 2 April 1988

Most League wins in a season
29 in 38 matches, FA Premier League, 2004-05 & 2005-06

Fewest League wins in a season
5 in 42 matches, First Division, 1978-79.

Didier Drogba scored a hat-trick in the record 8-0 walloping of Wigan

ALL SQUARE

Record draw

5-5 v. West Ham United, First Division, 17 December 1966

Most League draws in a season

18 in 42 matches, First Division, 1922-23.

Fewest League draws in a season

3 in 38 matches, FA Premier League, 1997-98

Longest sequence of League draws

6 20 August 1969 - 13 September 1969

OUCH!

Record League defeat

1-8 v. Wolverhampton Wanderers, First Division, 26 September 1953

Record FA Cup defeat

0-6 v. Sheffield Wednesday, Round 2 Replay, 5 February 1913

Record League Cup defeat

2-6 v. Stoke City, Round 3 Replay, 22 October 1974

Record European defeat

0-5 v. Barcelona, Fairs Cup, semi-final replay, 25 May 1966

Record Champions League defeat

1-5 v. Barcelona, in quarter-final second leg, 18 April 2000

Longest sequence of League defeats

7 1 November 1952 - 20 December 1952

Most League defeats in a season

27 in 42 matches, First Division 1978-79.

Fewest League defeats in a season

1 in 38 matches, FA Premier League, 2004-05.

Bobby Tambling scored two late goals in the 5-5 draw with West Ham

RECORD POINTS

Most points earned in a season (3 for a win)
99 in 42 matches, Second Division, 1988-89.

Fewest points earned in a season (3 for a win)
42 in 42 matches, First Division, 1987-88.

Most points earned in a season (2 for a win)
57 in 38 matches, Second Division, 1906-07

Fewest points earned in a season (2 for a win)
20 in 42 matches, First Division, 1978-79.

CLEAN SHEETS

Most clean sheets in one season
34 in 59 matches, (2004-05)

Fewest clean sheets in one season
2 in 47 matches, (1960-61)

Most League clean sheets in one season
25 in 38 matches, FA Premier League, 2004-05

Most consecutive clean sheets during a season
10 18 December 2004 to 12 February 2005

Most clean sheets by an individual goalkeeper
208 Peter Bonetti (1959-79)

Most clean sheets by an individual goalkeeper in a season
28 Petr Cech, (2004-05)

Most Premier League clean sheets by an individual goalkeeper in one season
21 Petr Cech, (2004-05)

Most consecutive clean sheets by an individual goalkeeper
9 William Foulke (1905-06)

Peter Bonetti, unbeaten in a Chelsea club record 208 matches

Record transfer fees paid

	To	Fee	Year
1 Andriy Shevchenko	Milan	£30.8m	2006
2 Michael Essien	Lyon	£24.4m	2005
3 Didier Drogba	Marseille	£24.0m	2004
4 S. Wright-Phillips	Man City	£21.0m	2005
5 Ricardo Carvalho	Porto	£19.9m	2004
6 Yuri Zhirkov	CSKA Moscow	£18.0m	2009
7 Ramires	Benfica	£17.0m	2010
8 Damien Duff	Blackburn	£17.0m	2003
9 Hernan Crespo	Inter Milan	£16.8m	2003
10 Claude Makelele	Real Madrid	£16.8m	2003

Record transfer fees received

	From	Fee	Year
1 Arjen Robben	Real Madrid	£24.0m	2007
2 Tore Andre Flo	Rangers	£12.0m	2000
3 Wayne Bridge	Manchester City	£10.0m	2009
4 S. Wright-Phillips	Manchester City	£8.5m	2008
5 Eidur Gudjohnsen	Barcelona	£8.0m	2006
6 Tiago	Lyon	£6.8m	2005
7 Ricardo Carvalho	Real Madrid	£6.7m	2010
8 Scott Parker	Newcastle United	£6.5m	2005
9 Chris Sutton	Celtic	£6.0m	2000
10 Robert Huth	Middlesbrough	£6.0m	2006

Premier League/European competition records

Fewest goals conceded in a League season
15 in 38 matches, Premier League, 2004-05 (English top flight record)

Fewest goals conceded at home in a League season
6 in 19 matches, Premier League, 2004–05 (English top flight record)

Fewest goals conceded away in a League season
9 in 19 matches, Premier League, 2004–05 (English top flight record)

Most consecutive clean sheets at the start of a season
6 Premier League, 14 August 2005 - 17 September 2005 (English top flight record)

Most goals in a Premier League season
103 Premier League, 2009-10 (Premier League record)

Longest sequence of unbeaten home league matches
86 Premier League, 20 March 2004 - 26 October 2008 (English record)

Highest aggregate scoreline in European competition
21-0 v Jeunesse Hautcharage, Cup Winners' Cup, 1st Round, 29 September 1971
(European record)

Most consecutive League away wins
11 Premier League, April 5 2008 - December 22, 2008 (English top flight record)

THE BRIDGE BOSSES

John Tait Robertson (1905–06)
William Lewis (1906–07 caretaker)
David Calderhead (1907–33)
Leslie Knighton (1933–39)
Billy Birrell (1939–52)
Ted Drake (1952–61)
Tommy Docherty (1961–67)
Dave Sexton (1967–74)
Ron Suart (1974–75)
Eddie McCreadie (1975–77)
Ken Shellito (1977–78)
Danny Blanchflower (1978–79)
Geoff Hurst (1979–81)
Bobby Gould (1981)
John Neal (1981–85)
John Hollins (1985–88)
Bobby Campbell (1988–91)
Ian Porterfield (1991–93)
David Webb (1993)
Glenn Hoddle (1993–96)
Ruud Gullit (1996–98)
Gianluca Vialli (1998–2000)
Graham Rix & Ray Wilkins (2000 caretakers)
Claudio Ranieri (2000–04)
Jose Mourinho (2004–07)
Avram Grant (2007–08)
Luiz Felipe Scolari (2008–09)
Ray Wilkins (2009 caretaker)
Guus Hiddink (2009)
Carlo Ancelotti (2009–)

Jose Mourinho, the 'Special One' who was sensationally successful when occupying the Chelsea hot seat.

CHELSEA'S ALL-TIME LEAGUE FINISHING POSITIONS

Season	Division	P	W	D	L	F	A	Points	Position
1905-06	Division Two	38	22	9	7	90	37	53	3rd
1906-07	Division Two	38	26	5	7	80	34	57	2nd
1907-08	Division One	38	14	8	16	53	62	36	13th
1908-09	Division One	38	14	9	15	56	61	37	11th
1909-10	Division One	38	11	7	20	47	70	29	19th
1910-11	Division Two	38	20	9	9	71	35	49	3rd
1911-12	Division Two	38	24	6	8	64	34	54	2nd
1912-13	Division One	38	11	6	21	51	73	28	18th
1913-14	Division One	38	16	7	15	46	55	39	8th
1914-15	Division One	38	8	13	17	51	65	29	19th
1919-20	Division One	42	22	5	15	56	51	49	3rd
1920-21	Division One	42	13	13	16	48	58	38	18th
1921-22	Division One	42	17	12	13	40	43	46	9th
1922-23	Division One	42	9	18	15	45	53	36	19th
1923-24	Division One	42	9	14	19	31	53	32	21st
1924-25	Division Two	42	16	15	11	51	37	47	5th
1925-26	Division Two	42	19	14	9	76	49	52	3rd
1926-27	Division Two	42	20	12	10	62	52	52	4th
1927-28	Division Two	42	23	8	11	75	45	54	3rd
1928-29	Division Two	42	17	10	15	64	65	44	9th
1929-30	Division Two	42	22	11	9	74	46	55	2nd
1930-31	Division One	42	15	10	17	64	67	40	12th
1931-32	Division One	42	16	8	18	69	73	40	12th
1932-33	Division One	42	14	7	21	63	73	35	18th
1933-34	Division One	42	14	8	20	67	69	36	19th
1934-35	Division One	42	16	9	17	73	82	41	12th
1935-36	Division One	42	15	13	14	65	72	43	8th

Season	Division	P	W	D	L	F	A	Points	Position
1936-37	Division One	42	14	13	15	52	55	41	13th
1937-38	Division One	42	14	13	15	65	65	41	10th
1938-39	Division One	42	12	9	21	64	80	33	20th
1946-47	Division One	42	16	7	19	69	84	39	15th
1947-48	Division One	42	14	9	19	53	71	37	18th
1948-49	Division One	42	12	14	16	69	68	38	13th
1949-50	Division One	42	12	16	14	58	65	40	13th
1950-51	Division One	42	12	8	22	53	65	32	20th
1951-52	Division One	42	14	8	20	52	72	36	19th
1952-53	Division One	42	12	11	19	56	66	35	19th
1953-54	Division One	42	16	12	14	74	68	44	8th
1954-55	Division One	42	20	12	10	81	57	52	1st
1955-56	Division One	42	14	11	17	64	77	39	16th
1956-57	Division One	42	13	13	16	73	73	39	13th
1957-58	Division One	42	15	12	15	83	79	42	11th
1958-59	Division One	42	18	4	20	77	98	40	14th
1959-60	Division One	42	14	9	19	76	91	37	18th
1960-61	Division One	42	15	7	20	98	100	37	12th
1961-62	Division One	42	9	10	23	63	94	28	22nd
1962-63	Division Two	42	24	4	14	81	42	52	2nd
1963-64	Division One	42	20	10	12	72	56	50	5th
1964-65	Division One	42	24	8	10	89	54	56	3rd
1965-66	Division One	42	22	7	13	65	53	51	5th
1966-67	Division One	42	15	14	13	67	62	44	9th
1967-68	Division One	42	18	12	12	62	68	48	6th
1968-69	Division One	42	20	10	12	73	53	50	5th
1969-70	Division One	42	21	13	8	70	50	55	3rd

Season	Division	P	W	D	L	F	A	Points	Position
1970-71	Division One	42	18	15	9	52	42	51	6th
1971-72	Division One	42	18	12	12	58	49	48	7th
1972-73	Division One	42	13	14	15	49	51	40	12th
1973-74	Division One	42	12	13	17	56	60	37	17th
1974-75	Division One	42	9	15	18	42	72	33	21st
1975-76	Division Two	42	12	16	14	53	54	40	11th
1976-77	Division Two	42	21	13	8	73	53	55	2nd
1977-78	Division One	42	11	14	17	46	69	36	16th
1978-79	Division One	42	5	10	27	44	92	20	22nd
1979-80	Division Two	42	23	7	12	66	52	53	4th
1980-81	Division Two	42	14	12	16	46	41	40	12th
1981-82	Division Two	42	15	12	15	60	60	57	12th
1982-83	Division Two	42	11	14	17	51	61	47	18th
1983-84	Division Two	42	25	13	4	90	40	88	1st
1984-85	Division One	42	18	12	12	63	48	66	6th
1985-86	Division One	42	20	11	11	57	56	71	6th
1986-87	Division One	42	13	13	16	53	64	52	14th
1987-88	Division One	40	9	15	16	50	68	42	18th
1988-89	Division Two	46	29	12	5	96	50	99	1st
1989-90	Division One	38	16	12	10	58	50	49	5th
1990-91	Division One	38	13	10	15	58	69	49	11th
1991-92	Division One	42	13	14	15	50	60	53	14th
1992-93	Premier League	42	14	14	14	51	54	56	11th
1993-94	Premier League	42	13	12	17	49	53	51	14th
1994-95	Premier League	38	13	15	14	50	55	54	11th
1995-96	Premier League	38	12	14	12	46	44	50	11th
1996-97	Premier League	38	16	11	11	58	55	59	6th

Season	Division	P	W	D	L	F	A	Points	Position
1997-98	Premier League	38	20	3	15	71	43	63	4th
1998-99	Premier League	38	20	15	3	57	30	75	3rd
1999-00	Premier League	38	18	11	9	53	34	65	5th
2000-01	Premier League	38	17	10	11	68	45	61	6th
2001-02	Premier League	38	17	13	8	66	38	64	6th
2002-03	Premier League	38	19	10	9	68	38	67	4th
2003-04	Premier League	38	24	7	7	67	30	79	2nd
2004-05	Premier League	38	29	8	1	72	15	95	1st
2005-06	Premier League	38	29	4	5	72	22	91	1st
2006-07	Premier League	38	24	11	3	64	24	83	2nd
2007-08	Premier League	38	25	10	3	64	26	85	2nd
2008-09	Premier League	38	25	8	5	68	24	83	3rd
2009-10	Premier League	38	27	5	6	103	32	86	1st

Art Turner 2010

A final word of thanks to Terry Baker of A1 Sporting Speakers for making this book possible, and a particular thank you to writer Norman Giller and his sports historian son, Michael, for helping me put it together. Norman, as you will learn on the following page, is one of the most prolific authors in the country. You can find out more on his website at www.normangillerbooks.co.uk

He and Terry are planning a series of books that you can learn about on Terry's website at www.a1sportingspeakers.com

Thank you, too, to outstanding artist Art Turner for his graphic illustrations. Lastly, a great big thank you to YOU for reading my book. I hope you found it informative as well as fun. If you like it, tell other Chelsea supporters ... if not, tell me. If you dare :-)